Reasons Not to Worry

Reasons Not to Worry

How to Be Stoic in Chaotic Times

BRIGID DELANEY

An Imprint of HarperCollins*Publishers*

HarperCollins books may be purchased for educational, business, or sales promotional use. For information, please email the Special Markets Department at SPsales@harpercollins.com.

Originally published in Australia in 2022 by Allen & Unwin.

FIRST U.S. EDITION

Library of Congress Cataloging-in-Publication Data has been applied for.

ISBN 978-0-06-331482-5

23 24 25 26 27 LBC 5 4 3 2 1

'It takes great courage to see the world in all its tainted glory, and still to love it.'

—Oscar Wilde

'Accept the things to which fate binds you, and love the people with whom fate brings you together, but do so with all your heart.'

—Marcus Aurelius

'These are times in which a genius would wish to live. It is not in the still calm of life, or in the repose of a pacific station, that great characters are formed. The habits of a vigorous mind are formed in contending with difficulties. Great necessities call out great virtues.'

—Abigail Adams, Letter to John Quincy Adams, 19 January 1780

Contents

Introduction

What a time to be alive! That's what I said every day as I hunched over my laptop, weak-eyed from looking at the screen and anxious from the news pouring through it, pounding me from all corners of the world. It felt—*feels*—as if we are in a permanent state of crisis, where one seismic global event folds into another, without pause for any of us to reorient ourselves to our ever-shifting, increasingly bleak reality.

The chaos on the outside we can catalogue well enough—a climate crisis, a pandemic, ongoing racism, rising inequality and soaring cost of living, wars, an increase in mental health problems—and then there's burnout, increased addiction and substance misuse, enslavement to our phones, an eroded sense of common ground, abuse and hate on social media, a retreat to our homes, screens, silos, platforms and echo chambers, an existential malaise brought on by a lack of ritual, community or shared meaning in our lives.

Being human right now feels like being blasted with a high-pressure hose—it's just all sensation and force; too much, it seems, to open our eyes.

Yet, yet . . . they have been years of wonder, too. In the early days of the pandemic there was an almost manic sense that *something was happening*. Briefly partitions between people—friends and strangers—fell and in came a strange, almost giddy sociability. There was in those strange days of autumn 2020 a glimpse of a different way of being, if only we could let it flow in.

Making meaning has always been my way through. Meaning becomes a map—and a map can get you out. I thought that if I could extract meaning from these years of chaos and wonder, and work out how to best get through these times, then I could future-proof myself for what was ahead. Because what was ahead promised to be wild. Wilder, perhaps, than what had come before.

The only problem is that our culture didn't—and still doesn't—really equip us with meaning or a map for navigating these last few years. In our secular society, there is no religion or broadly agreed upon social and moral tools for rising to life's increasingly complex challenges. Instead we are left to make it up as we go along. But how do we find consistent meaning in a time of continual change? And how do we plant our feet on the ground and not get carried away by the anxiety that society is falling apart? In the face of chaos, how do we feel optimistic and act with purpose and agency? And what does it mean to be a good person and act ethically? There was nothing I could see in our current culture that was strong enough to provide a ballast.

I needed a strong dose of wisdom to get through this harrowing passage of time. But where to find it?

In my previous books exploring the internet and globalisation (*This Restless Life*) and the wellness industry (*Wellmania*), I'd also been on a quest looking for answers. With this book, I was also looking for something, but not *out there*. I was looking *inside*.

I was searching for the tools to develop an inner life—an inner fortitude that would serve me until the end. This wisdom would guide my intuition, how I treated people, how I navigated the world and how I coped with it all: disappointment and loss, joy and abundance. But it would work inwards too—creating meaning and a map, orienting a moral compass, and creating the ability to be calm and courageous during times of global chaos and in a chaotic personal life.

By happenstance (more of that later) I found the wisdom I'd been searching for, deep in the past, in the ancient Greco-Roman philosophy of Stoicism.

The Stoics, always useful, seemed even more necessary in March 2020.

They whispered from the past: 'We're here, we're here . . . we've always been here.'

And so into the past I went. I found a time not unlike our own—full of chaos, war, plagues, pestilence, treachery, corruption, anxiety, overindulgence and fear of a climate apocalypse. Those times were populated by people questing for the answers that we crave today. In ancient Stoicism I found people, just like us, longing to find meaning and connection, to feel whole and tranquil, to love and be loved, to have a harmonious family life, fulfilling and meaningful work, intimate and nourishing friendships, a sense of contributing to your community, belonging to something greater than yourself, a wonder at the natural world, flashes of deep awe, a head full of questions about how it all came to be, and, finally, coming to terms with letting it all go—at some point, not of your choosing.

'We're here, we're here . . . we've always been here.' And so it was to the Stoics I went, falling down the two millennia towards them—in a quest to find out if the old ways can help us now.

How I came to write this book and why

I first came across the philosophy of Stoicism in 2018, started researching it and writing about it for this book in 2019, and completed the project in mid-2022.

The period between starting and finishing this book was so strange, disordered, chaotic, unprecedented and so desperately requiring the thing I was writing about that the project seemed eerily preordained. Deep in the trough of the pandemic, knowing Stoicism became a gift. It was like being in a sci-fi novel where the hero is propelled into the future with a superpower that, if used correctly, will set her free.

But how I became immersed in these ancient teachings, which exist today (with a few notable exceptions) largely in fragments and in the notes of their students, was initially a matter of chance.

In September 2018, the editor of *The Guardian*—a colleague and good friend, Bonnie Malkin—forwarded me an enticing press release. The subject-line read: 'Want to be happy? Then live like a Stoic for a week.' Run by academics at Exeter University in the UK, this was an online experiment that involved around 7000 people trying to live like an ancient Stoic for a week, undertaking daily readings and discussions. Their happiness levels were tested at the start and the end of the week, with the university trying to ascertain whether the Stoic way of life caused a measurable shift in happiness. Maybe I could do a fun column on it, suggested Bonnie.

According to the Stoic week press release there were five principles to living like a Stoic for a week. Now, years later, I still refer to these principles regularly.

1. Acknowledge that you can't control much of what goes on in your life.
2. See that your emotions are the product of how you think about the world.
3. Accept that bad things are bound to happen to you from time to time, just as they do to everyone else.
4. See yourself as part of a larger whole, not an isolated individual; part of the human race, part of nature.
5. Think of everything you have as not your own, but simply on loan, that one day will be taken back.

One week was not long enough to learn Stoicism. It was a big undertaking. Many of the principles were complex with clauses and exceptions, weird rules and unfamiliar theories. Sometimes the writing was knotty; the syntax was tangled via time and translations, and you had to read a sentence out loud several times to unravel its meaning.

The column I wrote for *The Guardian* about my week as a Stoic was a meta piece about how difficult, but also how stoic, it was to do Stoic week with a hangover.

In short, I missed the point.

But something about the experience lingered. I went back the following year, determined to take Stoic week a bit more seriously. I assembled a group of friends to do it with me and we met up in person in Sydney and virtually, on WhatsApp, to discuss the daily readings and the application of various principles. Among this disparate group of people aged between 30 and 45 (including a Byron Bay real estate agent, a business journalist at *The Australian*, an activist for political organisation GetUp!, a law student and a trainee priest), there was a hunger for the rules, the rigour and the logic that Stoicism promised. The Stoics had ˇa penchant for looking life in the face, seeing it for what it was, loving it fiercely anyway (despite everything . . . because of everything) and then finally—letting go.

It was the Stoics' hard, unarguable wisdom, their determination to face up to unpleasant things—to *reality*—that made me admire Stoicism, even if I struggled to sometimes *get* it.

In order to get it, I'd need longer than a week. My second year of Stoic week concluded. My WhatsApp group disbanded. I was left with the promise of a new way of seeing the world, a new way of being, that was in fact a Very Old Way of Being. But I needed someone to learn from, argue against and test the ideas in real time—a Stoic friend and mentor.

In this book, that's what I hope I will be to you. But first let's go back to the start and meet who it was for me.

In July 2019, I met an old friend, Andrew, for lunch. Andrew was in the corporate world, but a chance meeting at a book launch led to a friendship based on a love of discussing and debating ideas—often from opposing points of view. At lunch I explained I had been doing Stoic week. The teachings were complicated, dense and to my mind—softened by the fast food of Twitter spats and culture wars—they had an austerity and severity that wasn't easily digestible to the modern, distracted and discursive mind.

But something about Stoicism appealed to Andrew and in the weeks before we saw each other again he made a study of it and decided, in lieu of religion and despite the deep-rooted moral relativism of our age, that Stoicism was for him. Over drinks in a Surry Hills pub, he was full of enthusiasm about how it had helped him in parenting, in business and in dealing with colleagues. He was more methodical and organised than me—and far less liable to follow the latest wellness craze.

He told me what he found appealing about Stoicism, 'I like that it is a framework for living that is intellectual, that is reasoned—and I like that it is quite practical. The ideals that it sets up are achievable ideals, which recognise our strengths and weaknesses as humans— rather than holding us up to an ideal that we might struggle with and defining success as something unattainable for most people.'

But was Stoicism for me? I had a very different temperament. I was more rash, running on the energy of chaos. Could Stoicism work for both of us? Or did it suit only particular personality types? It was mid-2019 and I was in between travel writing assignments and book projects, so I thought: what's to lose? My rational self told me I might as well give it a go. My intuition told me I might actually need it.

What followed was two years of discussion, argument, reading and application of Stoic philosophy to our everyday lives—including work, love, relationships, parenting, health, wellbeing, fitness, mortality, politics, desire, responsibility, pet ownership, social media, mental health, money and ambition.

With this informal study I made a number of striking discoveries. That this pre-Christian philosophy seemed much more modern than Christianity—and much more egalitarian, inclusive of women and without a hierarchy (you could seek to attain the Stoic equivalent of sainthood—which is to be a Stoic sage, but so far I don't know anyone who has claimed that mantle). Rather than the narrow, self-disciplined idea of the Stoic being a self-reliant island, Stoics were actually deeply engaged in the idea of a society and community life. And that their view of nature and the cosmos was ecstatic, complex and profound—with the wild shards of paganism still embedded in their writing.

The Stoics also articulated the mood that we should aspire to as our default setting—*ataraxia* (literally, 'without disturbance')—a carefully calibrated state of tranquillity that is not happiness, or joy, or any of the ecstatic states found in religious or mystical experiences, or in the more modern highs of falling in love or taking cocaine. Instead, ataraxia is a state of contentment or peace where the world can be falling in around your ears, but your equilibrium is undisturbed.

Most of all I admired Stoicism for its clear-eyed view of humanity—always realistic, never cynical. There was no God in the sky that was going to come down and save you, and no afterlife. We only have ourselves and each other—and flawed as we all are, that is enough. But because we only have each other and ourselves, the philosophy demanded a sort of rising up to this challenge—requiring that you do your best, be rational, strive to be virtuous (more on what this means later), live according to your nature and treat others well, as you would your brothers and sisters. That is all that you can do and all that can be done.

The Stoics were realistic about our limits. They advised that, although you may want to try to persuade others to do what you want them to do or act how you want them to act, this is ultimately beyond your control. So don't waste your energy trying to change people.

The Stoics were also clear-eyed about death. They thought of it every day because they knew they were dying every day. The Stoics knew that it was important to honour the dead, but also not to use up too much of your life and your energy in grief. When my friends are knocked apart by grief, wanting some sort of guide through the unfamiliar netherworld of experience, it is the works of the Stoics, from around 2000 years ago, that I press upon them.

Over the course of writing this book, Stoicism got under my skin. Not all at once but slowly. I started using the philosophy in tricky situations and found it provided a framework not only for my own actions, but as a way of making sense of the world as a whole. I came to see Stoicism as a cradle-to-grave philosophy that I could use for my whole life. I could even use it at death.

At the midpoint in this process, a pandemic came along—a thing that gave the study Andrew and I were doing (with its plagues and pestilences and preparation for death) an eerie resonance. I was in Cambodia when Covid started to bite: Angkor Wat's massive car park deserted except for a few anxious, underworked rickshaw drivers; the ancient ruins burnished golden in a dawn glow; a lone Buddhist nun begging for alms; ravens nesting among the ruins; the place empty of tourists. I flew back to Sydney and, a week later, the borders shut. For a while—in the early days of the pandemic when everyone was scrambling and confused and jobs were lost and there were fears about door handles and washing of groceries—I was sought out by friends as a sort of interlocutor of the Ancients. They asked me: what would a Stoic do? Inject this Stoicism directly into my veins, they would say.

For a time I took this channelling seriously—setting up an Instagram account that gave Stoic advice in the form of easily digestible Zen-like koans. But behind the almost self-helpy lines from Marcus Aurelius, Epictetus or Seneca, there lay a dense and important theory, a map of how to live in this territory of troubled times.

Ultimately I found Stoicism to be incredibly helpful and surprisingly practical. It not only helped me to keep calm during the pandemic but it gave me a reason to get through my days beyond baking. Even more than that, Stoicism turned out to be personally transformative. It was as French philosopher Jean-Paul Sartre promised: a 'philosophy directed towards a total existential transformation of the individual; a philosophy that might teach him how to live'. Which is another way of saying, Stoicism can change your life—as it did mine.

I owe the teachings a great debt. And I feel close to my teachers, even though they are long dead.

The Stoic philosophers you'll meet in these pages—Epictetus, Seneca and Marcus Aurelius—lived hundreds of years ago but in many ways they are so similar to us, their concerns and anxieties so modern, I feel like they are only a breath away. I turn around and I can see them.

I didn't totally drink the Kool-Aid. I chafed against some of the Stoic teachings—and disagreements flared up occasionally when I met with Andrew. Was it possible to be happy or was the best we could hope for contentment? And what about emotion? And desire? How could these things be controlled? It wasn't just mind over matter—there was these things called hormones! What about neural pathways? The unconscious?

And both of us were united in our concern that Stoicism's emphasis on responsibility for one's own character and acknowledgement of the ultimate smallness of our spheres of influence meant that social justice and agitation for societal change had no place for a practising Stoic.

Andrew and I walked, talked, argued, read—and tried to work it all out. In the second half of 2020, we were neighbours in the small Sydney beachside suburb of Tamarama and took regular walks along the cliffs of Bondi and Bronte. After exchanging some pleasantries, we'd drop into it: the philosophy. What does it mean to have a good character? What is courage? Where do we go when we die? How do you control anger? How do you feel about giving without getting something in return? It was only after a couple of months of these walks, that I realised what I was trying to do: I was trying to work out how best to live.

Much of this book is a product of those discussions.

How Stoicism worked for me

I am not a philosopher or academic. I am a journalist who for two decades has worked on a general news beat, which often involves taking complex concepts and trying to break them down for readers.

I don't consider myself an expert. There are plenty of other people who have written more rigorous, academic and complex guides to Stoicism. You'll find their work referred to in these pages.

Instead, this book is the result of an experiment: applying some of the main Stoic principles to a 21st-century life—and seeing if any of them stick.

I'm happy to report that they do.

Who were the Stoics?

There are three main Stoic philosophers whom you'll meet in this book. They are Seneca (c. 4 BC–AD 65), Epictetus (AD c. 50–c. 135) and Marcus Aurelius (AD 121–180). All three Stoics are from a period known as the Roman Stoa—or late period of Stoicism.

They are important because their writing survived more or less intact, while the teachings from the earlier Greek period (around the early third century BC) have only been found in fragments.

Each of the three Stoics referred to in this book brings something different to the table. Epictetus came from harsh circumstances. He was born a slave, is said to have been lamed by a former master, and, once freed, taught philosophy. His lectures were recorded by a student called Arrian and were compiled into the *Enchiridion* (Greek for 'handbook'), a plain-speaking, powerful foundation document for the practice of Stoicism.

Seneca rose to become rich and powerful, a powerbroker and a player. He was Emperor Nero's tutor, a playwright, a political adviser and one of the wealthiest men in the Roman empire. He was published widely and much of his work remains available today. Scholars debate whether he was a hypocrite as he had a lavish lifestyle and worked for a dictator—but I will leave those debates to the historians. He was an excellent writer and his books of Stoic advice, particularly *Moral Letters to Lucilius,* feel as fresh today as they were in Roman times. *Letters* (the modern title) is a collection of 124 letters that Seneca wrote, after he had retired from working for Nero, to his younger friend Lucilius. Containing moral advice, the collection returned to prominence during the pandemic.

And finally Marcus Aurelius, once the most powerful man in the world. The philosopher emperor, who had studied Stoicism since he was young under the tutelage of some of the world's best teachers, had ample opportunity to put philosophy into practice. Although he wanted for nothing, he lived in a time of war and plague, lost nine of his fourteen children and had long bouts of ill health.

His book *Meditations* regularly tops lists of the best books of all time. The Daily Stoic website notes that prominent Americans from presidents to quarterbacks have found inspiration in it, as well as CEOs, the English socialist Beatrice Webb and the former prime minister of communist China, Wen Jiabao. But *Meditations* was never intended for publication; it was Marcus Aurelius's private journal.

But first, let's go back to the early third century BC and the birth of Stoicism in Athens. This was an exciting time for thought, innovation and advances in metaphysics (science), ethics, medicine and logic. Rationality and reason ruled but great plagues, slavery, illness and violent deaths were a constant challenge to a tranquil life. People were looking for instruction and guidance on how to live and how to cope with harsh and sudden misfortune. There was a range of gods and deities—not just the twelve Olympians but also Titans and others—but people had begun to look to the study of philosophy to teach coping skills, leadership and how to behave ethically towards others.

Many of the ancient philosophical schools had their beginnings in Athens where a thriving philosophy scene originated from Plato and his student and then colleague Aristotle. In ancient Greece, you could pick and choose what school most interested you, then attend lectures and talks by the heads of those schools.

Not only was there the Stoic school, founded by Zeno of Citium in around 300 BC, but Aristotle's Lyceum was going strong. Epicurus was also setting up his own school in the countryside that focused on pleasure and communal living and the harder-edged, disciplined Cynics were also thriving at about the same time.

Stoicism began when Zeno of Citium, a merchant and native of modern-day Cyprus, was transporting a precious cargo of extremely rare and valuable purple dye (the raw materials that were used to dye robes Tyrian purple). He was shipwrecked and his misfortune was absolute: he was stranded, without money and all his goods were ruined. At a loss about what to do, he went to Athens and sat in a bookseller's shop. He asked the proprietor where one might find a good philosopher, when a man called Crates happened to walk past. Crates was a well-known philosopher from the Cynic school. The bookseller said 'follow that man'—and so Zeno did, both literally and figuratively. He became a student of Crates. After a few years of study, Zeno started his own school and adapted some of the Cynics' teachings to his own philosophy. His followers met under the painted porch, or 'stoa', a public place on one side of the agora, or marketplace, in the centre of the city. There they became known as the Stoics. Anyone could come and listen to Zeno lecture on topics from human nature to justice to law, education, poetry, rhetoric and ethics.

Zeno's popular public lectures—which his pupils Cleanthes and Chrysippus continued after he died—laid the first foundations of Stoicism as we have come to know it today. The same teachings travelled to Rome hundreds of years later and influenced many of the surviving texts by Seneca, Epictetus, Musonius Rufus, Cicero and Marcus Aurelius among others.

Early Stoicism certainly was not the hyper-masculine, dead white male, red pill thing that it is thought to be these days.

The early Greek Stoics had a fairly radical approach to equality. Well, radical for ancient times. They considered everybody with the ability to reason equal—free men, women, slaves—and all were encouraged to study philosophy. Greek Stoics were of the view that in an ideal city there would be equal citizenship for all virtuous human beings, and even advocated the removal of gender distinctions as created by differences in clothing. According to modern Stoic author Massimo Pigliucci, 'The Stoics were among the first cosmopolitans. They imagined an ideal society in *Zeno's Republic* . . . that looks like an anarchic utopia, where wise men and women live in harmony because they finally understood how to use reason for the betterment of humankind.' These early Greek Stoics believed in equality for all—not just men and women—but people of different nationalities. Take Epictetus, born enslaved in Asia Minor and loaded up in chains on a slave caravan to Rome when he was fifteen. The journey was horrific, and he went to auction as a cripple, having a smashed knee that was left untreated. Once freed later in life, he ended up becoming one of the most influential philosophers of the Roman period. Class and physical ability meant nothing without good character and the ability to reason.

Sadly not much of the work of the early Greek Stoics survived, except in small fragments. Much of what we learn about Stoicism theory and practice these days comes from the Roman Stoics.

Stoicism travelled from Athens to Rome in around 155 BC and became popular among the young Roman elite.

In Rome, the study of Stoicism was limited to men because of rigid customs and hierarchy. But Roman Stoic Musonius Rufus argued for women to be taught Stoicism, saying that anyone who possessed the five senses, plus reasoning power and moral responsiveness, should study philosophy.

Stoicism declined in popularity after the death of Marcus Aurelius in AD 180, and the rise of Christianity.

In more recent times, the word 'Stoic' has been flattened and bastardised, used to describe people who bottle up their emotions, repress their feelings and never cry. The original Stoics were not like that at all. They enjoyed life, loved others and were part of communities. They wanted to maximise joy and minimise negative thinking. They knew you couldn't stop life from throwing you curve balls, losses and grief—but they tried to react positively or neutrally to all the things that came their way. As a result, they were relaxed and not fearful, no matter what happened. Stoic philosophy provided a whole-of-life system that they could follow and that would serve them until they died.

Modern Stoicism

Today, Stoicism is undergoing a revival. Unlike religion, with its set orthodoxies and rules, Stoicism is pliable. It has no leader or cabal guarding its purity and it can't be co-opted by various sects or interest groups who claim it as their own. I found most popular references to Stoicism in places that had little resonance in my actual life: the military, sports, in the libertarian ethos of tech bros and in alt-right communities. How could I embrace a philosophy that had been embraced by people who did not embrace me? Yet the pliability of Stoicism—the fact that it has no leader and no flag, no building or membership or nation—is also the thing that is liberating about the philosophy. Embedded in the philosophy itself is room to move. Stoicism was deliberately left open to change and interpretation as knowledge, particularly in science, evolved. As Seneca put it: 'men who have made these Discoveries before us are not our Masters but our guides. Truth lies open for all; it has not yet been monopolised. And there is plenty of it left even for posterity to discover.'

As a woman, and also as a person outside philosophical circles, I didn't need permission to enter. I could go into the philosophy and, in the spirit of its innate flexibility, make it my own.

Part 1

THE ESSENTIALS

'Whatever can happen at any time can happen today.'

—Seneca

'Very little is needed to make a happy life; it is all within yourself, in your way of thinking.'

—Marcus Aurelius

'Misfortune weighs most heavily on those who expect nothing but good fortune.'

—Seneca

S toicism is, above all, a practical philosophy. It's extraordinarily useful in almost every situation—from missing a flight or having someone cut in front of you in traffic to getting a scary medical diagnosis or being dumped by your partner.

Stoicism has something to say about our relationships with all kinds of people, from our closest intimates to our worst enemies. It also addresses our relationship with nature and the cosmos.

And Stoicism provides tools for dealing with your own inner life. How do we navigate the storms, the darkness, the desires and the disappointments that haunt all of us? How do we cope with loss and grief? How do we live with ourselves when we have acted badly and are wrestling with our own failures and shortcomings? How do we love the life we have and the people we have surrounded ourselves with?

Stoicism has it all covered. But first, let's start at the end.

Be mortal

'Your days are numbered. Use them to throw open the windows of your soul to the sun. If you do not, the sun will soon set, and you with it.'
                                                    —Marcus Aurelius

'People are frugal in guarding their personal property; but as soon as it comes to squandering time they are most wasteful of the one thing in which it is right to be stingy.'   —Seneca

I was 29 when I was first viscerally struck by the inevitability of my own death (I had also been viscerally struck in the head). I was in the back of an ambulance, covered in blood, a stranger in a strange city, going to which hospital I did not know, all alone, with an uncertain outcome, and a great gashing, gushing wound to the skull.

I'd suffered a head injury after being mugged for my wallet in the back streets of Barcelona's port district, coming back from a club around 5 a.m. Foolishly I chased the mugger, almost caught him, when he pushed me away and into a wall that had a jagged exterior (was it a Gaudi? It *felt* like a Gaudi). My skull took the brunt, splitting open above my right temple.

There were a string of half-lit, dreamy moments: dawn; in the ambulance and racing down La Rambla in a daze; revellers going home, lurching across roads, slumped on benches; and the paper stand sellers and flower stall merchants, full of purpose, setting up for the day ahead. What else? Soft rain on the windshield, a smear of colour, Barrio Gótico, Plaza de Cataluña, a fountain, a corner turned, the streets widening, everything grey and golden and beautiful. I was full of love. I was detached.

I thought that I would likely die, even though there was so much more to do with my life and I was kinda still mostly young. Yet the certainty that I would die didn't really trouble me—I felt curiously relaxed. It was nothing personal, I understood. It was okay to die now. I'd had a good run, I was 29, almost 30, I'd not done it all, but I'd done enough . . .

As it turns out, I didn't die. I was lucky. Instead I ended up with a bunch of stitches (and later, and currently, a scar) and heightened levels of anxiety. Turning corners into unfamiliar streets, the dark places between the pools of streetlights, the quickening of footsteps behind me at night—these things scared me for a while until, at some barely perceptible point, I got out of the woods.

After a month or so, I stopped thinking about the assault itself and started interrogating my reaction in the back of the ambulance. Why was I so *relaxed* about dying? And would I feel the same way now that I'm older? There was only one way of knowing, and I didn't want to get as close to the edge again just to satisfy an intellectual curiosity.

But I knew that I certainly didn't feel relaxed or detached when people close to me died.

A few years after that time in Barcelona, an old friend died of an accidental overdose. It was a shock. That she could be so suddenly and arbitrarily removed from the world caused me and those she loved a lot of pain. But more than that—anger. To die young seemed terribly unjust. The natural order of things had been upended; an implied contract had been broken. You take a drug, but you always wake up . . . don't you?

My friend's death affected me much more deeply than my own glimpse of mortality. It provoked the first intimations that the universe is not a benevolent entity, is not a forever home—but more like a video game where players are summarily eliminated and the game keeps going. Or a chess game where pieces around you are taken and taken and taken and taken until it is your turn to be removed . . . Or the universe itself not being round but flat and someone can walk too close to the edge and just fall off, just slip away and you can't catch them (you didn't even see them fall!)—you can't bring them back. And the permanence of it! She was gone forever.

At her Catholic burial the family priest said we would all meet again in heaven, but I didn't believe that anymore. Doubt and consolation were with each other, that night, at the pub. I drank too much and the anger came spilling out and the only place to take it out on the street was with a nearby rubbish bin.

Furious, I started high kicking this metal rubbish bin, high-heeled feet creating a semi-satisfying impact, howling 'fuck you' over and over until two policewomen came out of nowhere and told me to stop. 'You've had too much chardonnay,' said one, which felt both damning and weirdly specific. Chardonnay? My grief, which felt large, unique, terrible, formal and Shakespearean, was witnessed by outsiders as the rantings of a woman who had had too much oaky wine.

In both cases—when I was injured and when my friend died—my reaction to mortality was instinctive, deeply primal and unadulterated by anything outside myself. My reactions were not tempered, measured or filtered through rationality, religion or philosophy. They came from the gut and felt ancient and universal. How could people bear this, to see death up close over and over and over again?

We all go through it sooner or later—that first shocking death of a friend or family member. And we all have our first brush with our own mortality. When we do, something shifts—like being told a terrible secret that we're all in on, in the end.

It is both the most shocking and the most natural of things to know that we—and everyone we love—are going to die.

But why does the first death feel like being let in on a secret?

Perhaps because for the most part we are not living in reality. Instead we are living in a society that likes to pretend we will never die, or grow sick and old. The *real* secret is not that we are going to die, but that we live in a culture that pretends we won't.

Our culture and these times runs on the algorithm of youth, a torrent of constantly moving images in our social media feeds that glorify the trivial, the next, the silly, the surface, the hot take, the meme, the shocking, the zeitgeist. I love the times we live in—they are not dull—but this constant fresh *content*, the constant refreshing of the page, each take hotter than the last, has its downside: that is, our culture is too immature to square up to death.

This lack of squaring up (looking life in the face) is everywhere. In our society we no longer have ritual or language or ways of being comfortable with death. Our screens are drenched in representations of violence, in actual violence, surrounded by death, yet we don't have the mechanisms (or the ritual or the poetry) to process our own mortality. One of the most perfect examples of this was when people started dying of Covid in large numbers in America, and President Trump spoke with a kind of incredulity that death was—like—*a thing*: 'I wish we could have our old life back. We had the greatest economy that we've ever had, and we didn't have death,' he said with a kind of stunned innocence. Wasn't that all of us?

We fight for a few extra years at the back end of life, throwing money, technology and medicine at buying more time, when, in fact, we do not appreciate the years we have while we are actually living them.

I often think of the excellent Kazuo Ishiguro book, *Never Let Me Go*. It's ostensibly about cloning and organ donation, but I read it as a parable of our own death denial (*we had the greatest economy that we've ever had, and we didn't have death*). The tragedy of *Never Let Me Go* is that the characters were created to die. And when they, and we the reader, find out this knowledge had been hidden from them in their childhood, the effect on the reader is a terrible melancholy. They will all meet their end. Why can't they just be allowed *to live*? And then—mic drop—there is the second realisation, more shocking than the first. This is *our fate* too, the fate of the reader! We too are born to die, at a time not of our choosing. Why can't *we* just be allowed to live on and on?

In a review of the book for *The Telegraph*, Theo Tait, wrote: 'Gradually, it dawns on the reader that *Never Let Me Go* is a parable about mortality. The horribly indoctrinated voices of the Hailsham students who tell each other pathetic little stories to ward off the grisly truth about the future—they belong to us; we've been told that we're all going to die, but we've not really understood.'

We've not really understood—but the Stoics spent their lives attempting to understand that they would die.

And then there's grief. We grieve alone, and often deeply, unsupported except for Facebook in memoriam sites and the GP's offer of antidepressants. How to do this thing, to deal with this pain—these shards of glass, this wall of fire, this icy steppe—that we all must pass through? The Stoics thought deeply about the question of mortality and grief—and wrote some of their most enduring works on it. Seneca put it like this in his book *On the Shortness of Life*: 'Learning how to live takes a whole life, and . . . It takes a whole life to learn how to die.'

What we *can* do is prepare for death. We can face reality. That sometimes grim, sometimes liberating task of preparing for death has always been available to us and yet we turn away. We do not *want* to prepare. There is still a superstition that runs deep into the marrow, that if we prepare, we are calling forth death ourselves, somehow willing it—a dark version of a vision board. We don't prepare, because in our magical thinking, we believe if we don't face death then no one we love, including ourselves, will die.

But prepare we must. For death is already happening to us in each passing moment. It's happening as I write these words, to all of us. Every day we are dying.

Awareness of the shortness of life, of our own and others' mortality is a keystone of Stoic philosophy. It is also crucial in taming some of the chaos that comes with grief, sudden losses and squaring with our own mortality.

So that is where we will start.

Ancient Stoic philosophers lived in perilous times. Mothers and their babies died in childbirth, diseases ravaged populations, there were plagues, massive inequality and slavery. If you were involved in politics, like Seneca, you had to be constantly on guard against your enemies who might try to kill you or have you exiled (Seneca was exiled twice and ordered to kill himself by his former employer, the emperor Nero).

In order to exist in some sort of tranquillity during highly uncertain times, the Stoics had to face reality: that is, they were mortals who were born to die.

For a Stoic, to be able to die well was intimately linked with being able to live well. If you realised how short and arbitrary life was, you didn't waste a second.

And by continually acknowledging the inevitability of death, by the time you reached the end of your life (whether that end came when you were young or old or in between) you wouldn't have the regrets that haunted people who acted as if they would live forever.

There were several tools Stoics used to contemplate and inoculate themselves against the shock of their mortality. By thinking of mortality often (giving them a small dose of the disease, like we do with a vaccine), the Stoics became used to the idea, so it wouldn't be so shocking when the end came. In other words, they prepared for the worst, often over a lifetime.

Imagine your friends dying

The Stoics believed that you should grieve your loved ones while they are living. They advised you to think of their death frequently while the person was still alive, in order to prepare for the inevitable.

Seneca said, 'Let us greedily enjoy our friends,' as we should also enjoy our children, 'because we do not know how long this privilege will be ours'.

When I first started learning about Stoicism, imagining people dying while they are still alive, oblivious to death and enjoying their life, sounded morbid. But as it is a practice embedded deep in the teaching of the three Roman Stoics I was studying (Seneca, Epictetus and Marcus Aurelius), I gave it a go.

The aim of the exercise is to treasure your friends in the here and now, rather than being full of sadness, grief and regret when they die.

Seneca says: 'Let us see to it that the recollection of those whom we have lost becomes a pleasant memory to us.' It is pleasant because we have fully appreciated them while they are still alive, and we are not wracked with suffering and taken by surprise when they die (a Stoic should not be surprised by death).

In order to prepare for grief the Stoics used a technique called negative visualisation, or *futurorum malorum præmeditatio* (Latin, literally meaning pre-studying bad future).

With negative visualisation, you imagine someone you love dearly dying the following day or that night. The time you are spending with them today is the last day they have on earth (or maybe the last day *you* have on earth). It makes the time spent with them incredibly precious if you acknowledge that it is finite.

I still have a very clear memory of last seeing my schoolfriend before she died. She was working in a cafe in a coastal town, and I popped in to see her. I sat in a booth as she worked around me, stopping in quiet times to chat. I had a sausage roll from the bakery across the road, and asked her if I could eat food not purchased in the cafe. 'Of course,' she said, laughing. 'Just hide it.' I ordered a coffee and sat there, happily, *discreetly*, munching on my contraband sausage roll while she came and went, the conversation breaking so she could serve customers. But when we did talk, I noticed my friend was uncharacteristically anxious. I comforted her and tried to make her feel okay. But I wondered later, after she died—did I comfort her and support her as if it would be *the very last time I saw her*? No. It was not quality time. I was trying to talk to her while she was working in a busy cafe. It was a fond but distracted encounter. This is understandable. I had thought there would be many, many more conversations—and many, many more storms (but also calm ports) for both of us. The need to really make the moment special, the urgency of it—was not there.

But the Stoics say we should treat every encounter, with everyone, particularly people close to us, as if it may be the last. It's a hard pill to swallow—particularly if you are contemplating the death of a child, and particularly if that child is your own.

Preparing for the death of your children

The most chilling passage of Stoicism (or perhaps any in any work of literature) is that of Epictetus advising students to practise negative visualisation about the death of their child. 'Remind yourself that what you love is mortal . . . At the very moment you are taking joy in something, present yourself with the opposite impressions. What harm is it, just when you are kissing your little child, to say: "Tomorrow you will die", or to your friend similarly: "Tomorrow one of us will go away, and we shall not see one another anymore?"'

Read the Epictetus passage cold, without knowing Stoicism and you'd be forgiven for thinking that the Stoics were monsters:

Tomorrow you will die.

Tomorrow one of us will go away, and we shall not see one another anymore.

(It's not just the Stoics. There are also echoes of this in Christianity with a prayer my nanna used to say with me when I was a child: 'Now I lay me down to sleep, I pray the Lord my soul to keep /If I die before I wake/I pray the Lord my soul to take.')

The Stoics believed that life is random and arbitrary, bad things happen even if you take all precautions, and death is waiting for all of us—and not at a time of our choosing. A disease can take your child, or an accident can take your friend—just like an accidental overdose took my friend—or a blow to the head can almost kill you— as it might have killed me in Spain.

By acknowledging our precarious reality and place on this planet, the Stoics hoped that when the worst happened, the negative visualisation would rob the moment of its full power.

Going too far with negative visualisation

Would negative visualisation help with making death seem more inevitable and natural? And could it improve my relationships in the present, by making me appreciate loved ones more while they are still alive?

I decided to give negative visualisation a shot but the process can be hard to get right. It's like a recipe—too much thinking of the worst-case scenario can tip you into anxiety, while too little might not be enough to shift your thinking, and really future-proof you for when the worst happens.

Andrew and I met up in Sydney to discuss how we were faring with our Stoic practices just after Christmas in 2019. Christmas and time with family always lends itself to situations where Stoicism can come in very handy—and that particular Christmas was no exception. I was in the early days of experimenting with negative visualisation and the only thing I had succeeded in was becoming incredibly anxious about everyone I loved dying.

There I was sitting around the Christmas lunch table surrounded by generations of my nearest and dearest kin, imagining everyone being killed in a freak ten-car pile-up on the way home, or being poisoned by bad seafood or a bushfire roaring towards the house . . . It was horrible.

Back in Sydney, Andrew counselled me to use negative visualisation habitually but fleetingly—just having a 'flash' of thought of someone dying, rather than dwelling excessively on it. He used it a lot and agreed that 'sometimes it can be hard—it's never nice to think through bad scenarios, but once you've done it, you tend to be grateful for any outcome you get'. He said doing it was 'like an insurance policy—you reconcile yourself to any outcome, even the bad ones'.

'You should still be enjoying family occasions, but just remember that not everyone might be together in the same way again,' he said.

What he advised proved prescient.

The pandemic started in earnest in Australia a few months later, in March 2020, and borders quickly shut. In lockdown, we were unable to go more than 5 kilometres from home or visit family. Maybe that

2019 Christmas, the one that I had been negatively visualising as *being the last*, would actually *be* the last?

It turned out not to be the last but not every family was so lucky. Many families (including half-a-dozen people I know) lost loved ones in those two years and were unable to attend funerals or be with relatives in their last days.

After being separated from my family, I have found the time we have been able to reunite is extra special because I no longer take it for granted. I used negative visualisation regularly but fleetingly— as Andrew advised—over the two years my family was separated by border closures. When there were brief respites in lockdown, and I was able to see my parents, I imagined that each visit would be the last time and that one of us would die soon after. Using this brief flash of imagining, I tried to make the most of each visit.

But as my family are still alive, it's impossible to tell whether my Stoic experiments of negative visualisation would have lessened the pain had they died during lockdown. Time will tell. We're all going to die, sooner or later, so I'll know eventually—unless I die first. But treating every occasion with my parents as if it will be the last has sharpened my enjoyment of their company.

Remove fear—think of your own death frequently

As well as thinking about the death of others when you practise negative visualisation, you should also contemplate your own death.

The Stoics were realistic about the prospect of death and their allotted time on earth. They realised they couldn't control death, but they *could* control how they thought about it. Epictetus says: 'I cannot escape death, but at least I can escape the fear of it.'

The Stoics escaped the fear of death by routinely acknowledging the reality of it. When a general returned in glory to ancient Rome, he was accompanied in his procession through the streets by a slave whose job it was to remind him that his triumph would not last forever. '*Memento mori*,' the slave whispered into the general's ear: 'Remember you will die.'

The idea is to habituate yourself to thoughts of your own mortality. You can't begin to properly contemplate death if you live in constant terror of it. By reminding ourselves regularly that we will die, we sharply bring into focus the one thing that really matters: the present moment—the time that we have. When we realise that our moments are slipping away with unceasing constancy, we come to realise how short life actually is.

In *On the Shortness of Life*, Seneca wrote:

> You are living as if destined to live forever; your own frailty never occurs to you; you don't notice how much time has already passed, but squander it as though you had a full and overflowing supply—though all the while that very day which you are devoting to somebody or something may be your last. You act like mortals in all that you fear, and like immortals in all that you desire . . .

Nothing has really changed since Seneca wrote these words. We still live 'as if destined to live forever'. We put off things we really want to do until retirement, or we think we can take a break only when we earn a certain amount of money, or we borrow a lot of money to have a big mortgage in a posh suburb—not really contemplating that it ties us to working hard, perhaps in an industry we hate, for another 30-plus years.

Marcus Aurelius cautioned: 'Do not act as if you were going to live ten thousand years. Death hangs over you. While you live, while it is in your power, be good.'

In ancient times, it was as it is now: so many of us never actually begin our lives. We're too busy working and making money, promising that one day we'll stop and properly rest and luxuriate in the present. Seneca nailed it when he said:

You will hear many people saying: 'When I am fifty I shall retire into leisure; when I am sixty I shall give up public duties.' And what guarantee do you have of a longer life? Who will allow your course to proceed as you arrange it? Aren't you ashamed to keep for yourself just the remnants of your life, and to devote to wisdom only that time which cannot be spent on any business? How late it is to really begin to live just when life must end!'

We are masters at putting things off, getting lost in work and busyness. All the while time and life are passing, yet we seem barely aware of how we *do* time. Thinking about our own death forces us to concentrate on the time we have.

Time is our most valuable currency

Stoics were highly attuned to time, seeing it as the only true currency we have. It is also our most democratic currency: everyone—no matter their material wealth—is given an allotment of time (although how much varies, and extra time is one thing money can't buy).

I waste torrents of time. Daily, I get sucked into the internet and spend hours a day engaged in things that don't matter or petty disputes that I won't remember next week. It's not really work, but nor is it meaningful leisure, nor is it contemplation and relaxation. An ancient Stoic would see excessive use of the internet as an extremely poor use of time. Would I take a bunch of money and just throw it in the bin? No. But somehow I squander my time online without a second thought.

Time-wasting is not a new problem. Wrote Seneca nearly 2000 years ago: 'Can you show me even one person who sets a price on his time, who knows the worth of a day, who realises that every day is a day when he is dying? In fact, we are wrong to think that death lies ahead: much of it has passed us by already, for all our past life is in the grip of death.'

In life, money will come and go but time is always running out. We can't borrow more time or create more time. We have what we have, and it is always dwindling, never accumulating. Once you truly realise that, the way you organise your life changes. If you see time as the most valuable thing you have, you may feel less liable to fill your day with meetings that don't create meaningful outcomes or less willing to spend a sunny Saturday in bed nursing a hangover or less likely to spend a weekend away with people whose company you don't enjoy. We squander time because we think we have an unlimited supply of it. In some deluded corner of our minds, we think we are going to live forever.

Of course, I am telling you nothing new here—there have been alarms sounding about our addictions to money, work and work-related status for years now. But so many factors, particularly the nature of our capitalist system, keep us bound to this same exhausted dream.

Many people in the gig economy work seven days a week, ten hours a day—collecting bits of money from arrangements with various apps. And in the white-collar world, even when we are not working, we carry our work with us. Our phones and emails tether us to the office so that even in our downtime we still have our work brains cranking.

People are realising there's got to be a better way to *do life*. That way may involve a reduction in income or security but, in return, you get your time back.

This rethinking of work is nothing new. There is a proud lineage of people reassessing their relationship with time and work that stretches back to the school of Epicureanism—a rival philosophy to early Greek Stoicism that encouraged participants to live communally, tend a garden and spend time in contemplation, leisure and the study of philosophy.

And in 1845 Henry David Thoreau worked out how much money (or how little) he would need to live a simple life of contemplation in the countryside. He did the sums and, for just over two years, he did his best to live harmoniously with nature in the Massachusetts woods.

Then came the hippies of the 1960s and the FIRE (financially independent, retire early) and van life movements of today. And now, after more than two years in a pandemic, we have a generation of people questioning the oversized role work plays in our lives.

Imagine if more of us elevated our *time* to be the central, organising principle in our lives? The result would be nothing less than a total revolution in how we live. We would wake up from this fog that we have been in for so long now, where we live as if we have all the time in the world, and put off what we really want to do until we retire (if we are actually lucky enough to retire) or reach this mysterious end point called 'one day'. One day you will travel more, or rest more, or read more, or write a book or play with your kids, or start a business or move to the country or start a family. *'How late it is to really begin to live just when life must end!'*

Recently I reflected on what were the happiest periods of my life. The one thing that these good times had in common was that they occurred when I was not rushed, when I had a lot of time. Wealth took on a different form. When I had a wealth of time, I was under-employed and didn't have much money. I also had anxiety about whether I would get work in the future. But looking back, having a wealth of time felt better and more magical than having a lot of money in the bank. I call them my Huckleberry days—after Mark Twain's great paean to the pleasures of leisure and endless swathes of time. ('It's lovely to live on a raft. We had the sky, up there, all speckled with stars, and we used to lay on our backs and look up at them, and discuss about whether they was made, or only just happened—')

Huckleberry days . . . Nothing-to-do afternoons and bright blue long twilights, biking around Berlin in 2008. I was scraping together a subsistence living freelancing travel stories, but I had so much time and my friends were similarly poor and rich on time, so we squandered it wisely, wandering around the city on bikes or on foot, stopping to play table tennis in the park, balancing a cheap beer on the edge of a table, or, if there were no tables free, flinging our bikes on the ground and lying beside them, reading books under a tree in the Tiergarten.

Then there were the two three-month stints in New York where I had cheap sublets in Park Slope, the Upper West side, Bushwick . . . and with no place to be or nowhere to go, I could just explore the greatest city in the world: afternoons spent at Prospect Park, flea markets in Hell's Kitchen, cycling along the High Line on a Citibike, walking Manhattan's grids with no destination in mind, a drink in a rooftop bar, the city alive and humming electric below.

Or even during the pandemic. In the first lockdown, my brother came to live with me in the country, 80 minutes inland from Melbourne. It was early autumn, the leaves were turning and we both had bikes. With everything shut, and nowhere to go, we'd go on long rides into the bush and up into the hills—stopping in small village shops to buy a drink or a pie, the roads eerily empty, an eagle circling over-head—venturing into the back roads where the bush thrummed with bird life and animals and insects, all oblivious to the panic and anxiety in the cities beyond.

And 2021, another lockdown, this time Sydney—and my friend Ivan and I would meet on the cliff path at Bondi and go on long walks. Sometimes we'd stop and sit on rocks and there'd be dolphins jumping through the air. Other times on the harbour-side we'd do the Hermitage walk, stopping at little bays along the way and swim-ming—and at sunset, rounding the path into Rose Bay, and stepping onto the beach, the sky would be on fire, briefly, vividly glowing red.

All these beautiful, glorious things—all these riches!—were free, the only cost being time.

Work—but make it meaningful

Huckleberry days are great but they need to be balanced with work and contribution.

The ancient Stoics believed you should work hard and take pride in what you do, but that work is only one part of life.

The Roman Stoics—Seneca, Marcus Aurelius and Epictetus—were hardly slackers, although the Greek Stoics might have levelled this charge at their rival school, the Epicureans, who were more removed from the world. Marcus Aurelius was the Roman emperor FFS!, and his reign was recognised as one of the most stable in the empire. Seneca was extremely prolific, writing hundreds of essays, plays and letters. And Epictetus, once freed from slavery, set up his own philosophy school late in life and adopted and raised a child right when he should have been kicking back into his retirement. The Stoics were cosmopolitan, powerful, dynamic, politically engaged and engaged in their communities—dropping out or resigning was not really their style.

But throughout their teachings is the belief that time—and how you spend it—is a much more important question than status and how much you get paid. Work for the Stoics was a way of building society, sharing ideas and contributing to the community, and the highest form of work was to be engaged in philosophy. Seneca said of philosophy and its value: 'it moulds and constructs the soul, it orders our life, guides our conduct, shows us what we should do and what we should leave undone—without it no one can live fearlessly or in peace of mind'.

The Stoics' interest in philosophy was not an abstract, academic exercise. Seneca, with a sort of New Testament Marxist Jesus vibe, attacked philosophers who went in for abstract intellectual concerns: 'There is no time for playing around. You have promised to bring help to the shipwrecked, the imprisoned, the sick, the needy, to those whose heads are under the poised axe. Where are you deflecting your attention? What are you doing?'

What are you doing, indeed?

The Stoics realised that life was short and believed that there was no afterlife; what mattered was our time here on earth. Seneca wrote that it is 'stupid to pray' in order to achieve something virtuous in life 'since you can obtain it from yourself'.

41

To work out how to live well, to really think about what a good life meant, was a solid investment in our one unique life. 'Do not act as if you have 10,000 years to throw away. Death stands at your elbow. Be good for something while you live and it is in your power,' wrote Marcus Aurelius.

STOIC EXERCISES IN REMOVING FEAR OF DEATH

To prevent the creeping fear of death as he ruled a far-flung, sprawling empire, Marcus Aurelius used to say to himself: 'Stop whatever you're doing for a moment and ask yourself: "Am I afraid of death because I won't be able to do this anymore?"'

This exercise is clarifying on two fronts. If the activity is something we enjoy and we are afraid of death because we will no longer get to engage in the activity (so perhaps spending time with your friends or family, hiking in the mountains, or your morning swim or coffee), then it is a signal that you should enjoy the moment, appreciate the activity and the people you are doing it with and really squeeze the most out of it you can.

If the activity is tedious or something you wouldn't miss—like housework, commuting, going to a job you hate—then there is less reason to be afraid of death because you won't have to do the loathed thing anymore.

Live each day as if it was your last

While Seneca counselled 'banishing all worry about death', he didn't mean you should then just forget about death altogether: he just meant that you shouldn't *worry* about it, rather you should *contemplate* it. There is a difference, as I found out when I started on my own negative visualisation exercises at Christmas. Instead, said Seneca, you should aim to live a life in a day—assuming that each day is your last.

'Let us prepare our minds as if we'd come to the very end of life. Let us postpone nothing. Let us balance life's books each day. The one who puts the finishing touches on their life each day is never short of time,' wrote Seneca.

VIEW FROM ABOVE

One way the Stoics prepared for death was to remind themselves of their place in the universe—that is, they occupied for a tiny amount of time, a tiny part of the cosmos.

Said Marcus Aurelius, 'How small a part of the boundless and unfathomable time is assigned to every man! For it is very soon swallowed up in the eternal. And how small a part of the whole substance! And how small a part of the universal soul! And on what a small clod of the whole earth you creep!'

We can often feel overwhelmed by how big the problems are in our life—and this zooming out, taking the view from above, can make us aware of the true nature of the smallness of our existence in the great span of time, and that our lives occupy but the measure of a grain of sand in the continuum of human history.

Anyone lucky enough to see Indigenous rock art from the world's oldest continuous culture, the Australian First Nations peoples, or to view the Egyptian pyramids, or gaze upon an ancient tree in the forests of northern California has probably experienced a mind-bending, humbling taste of the great span of time. Our lifetime is a speck in the world's history. And our problems that take up so much headspace and energy ultimately matter very little in the end.

Dealing with mortality first up is all a bit heavy—but the first part of my Stoicism journey was squaring with the fact that we all die, that we are dying every day, that everyone I love will die and that I will die too—at a time unknown, maybe sooner rather than later. After establishing that, after at least *acknowledging* that, I then turned my task to the next thing: learning how best to live.

Work out what matters

'Some things are in our control and others not.   —Epictetus

'The more we value things outside our control, the less control we have . . .'   —Epictetus

In late 2019 Andrew and I met one Sunday at his office in the city to discuss the Stoic reading we'd been doing and how to apply the principles to our lives.

It was an interesting—maybe fortuitous—time to learn from the old ways of coping in the world.

In those months in late 2019, there was a definite vibe shift. Massive bushfires were ringing Sydney, ash was falling from the sky as ancient forests burned, and billions of animals were incinerated. The sky was brown and the air acrid with smoke for months that summer. On the city streets, masks started appearing—the pointy N95s that filtered smoke and pollution, while children were kept home from school. In December, in a scene that felt emblematic of this new, dark age, I attended a launch at a pimped-out harbourside mansion for a new brand of rosé, smiling for selfies as large sheafs of ash fell from the sky and into our drinks.

We were all in our party dresses and chunky trainers, phones fully charged to maximise the Instagrammable location, only coughing a little bit although peoples' eyes were red and I noticed some fellow guests pulling on Ventolin inhalers. That day, Sydney's air quality was one of the worst in the world.

At the mansion there were a DJ, sommeliers and a chef, who explained in great detail the origin of the scallops on the canapés and recounted a recent, inspirational trip to Oaxaca. Later there was a wine tasting where we gathered around to swirl and spit. Every varietal had notes of bushfire.

The DJ played on but the tunes—Tones and I, Mark Ronson—were nervy, jangly and strangely discordant. The smell of the smoke had an almost chemical taint, and, in between glasses of rosé, I wondered about the alchemy at work in the commingling of the elements: the ancient forests and their animals turned to columns of ash, collapsed and drifting through the air, settling on the water and soil; and on my body after swimming in the murky sea that morning and now being swallowed as particles of ash floating in my wine at the party on the harbour's edge. ('At the end of the world,' I nervously joked with a friend.)

Influencers posed in the gloom on the jetty and by the swimming pool, seeing but refusing to see what was all around them: this red-raw sun, that dirty brown sky.

That was December 2019. It felt like the right time to be learning Stoicism.

The climate and old seasonal certainties were in freefall; there was no question now. But no one seemed to want to see reality—the razor's edge of the Anthropocene era that was unfolding in front of our eyes.

We didn't know then—how could we?—that the summer of 2019 would be the start of a string of dramatic and life-altering events linked to environmental destruction: fires, unbreathable air, a pandemic, floods. In a world that suddenly seemed to veer way more out of control than usual, working out what you *could control* in life was critical.

And that is where the study of Stoicism proved to be life changing— in teaching me how to face up to the reality of a rapidly degrading world, how I could be resilient in the face of these changes, and what I could do about the changes.

The ancient Stoics had a lot to say on reality—looking life in the face, and seeing it for what it was, and working with that reality.

The control test

The step the Stoics took first, before taking action, was to run everything through a basic test. Called the 'control test' or the Dichotomy of Control, the Stoics assessed what they could and could not control about a situation, and focused their attention on areas they could control.

This was the first Stoic principle we covered when we started meeting in Martin Place, at Andrew's office in the summer of 2019.

Andrew used a white board with stick figures and we drew on sheets of paper to break down what the control test looked like.

It looked a bit like this:

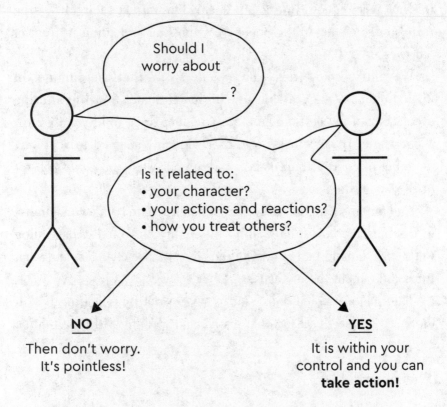

So fundamental is the control test to the practice of Stoicism that Epictetus set it out in the opening lines of the *Enchiridion*: 'Some things are in our control and others not. Things in our control are opinion, pursuit, desire, aversion, and, in a word, whatever are our own actions. Things not in our control are body, property, reputation, command, and, in one word, whatever are not our own actions.'

This passage is the cornerstone and the crucible of Stoic philosophy. It sets out the things we can control, which I have interpreted as being our character, the way we treat others and our actions and reactions. Epictetus then urges us to forget trying to control the rest. To do so is just a waste of time and energy.

This does not mean we shouldn't put any effort into something we can't directly control—like climate change. After all, Stoics were not passive people. Historically they were people of action: political leaders, emperors and soldiers. But they knew that even if they trained hard, acted with integrity, built alliances and put in a lot of effort, they couldn't control the outcome. They could only control their own character, own actions (and reactions) and how they treated others.

Initially, to my ears, this did not seem like a sufficient field of influence. Yet within this seemingly small ambit, the ancient Stoics led remarkable lives. Squaring up with not being able to control much in your external life did not lead to powerlessness—but rather the opposite. By focusing on your character, how you see the world and how you lead your life, you can harness where you have the true and realistic ability to effect change while also maintaining a state of personal tranquillity because you are not overly reliant on outcomes that are outside your control.

In those early sessions, Andrew explained that the control test was not just a useful decision-making tool, but *crucial* in applying Stoicism in his daily life. A central organising principle, the control test clarified everything and made making decisions and emotional investment easier to manage. In short, you work out first what you can control, and place your efforts there, and don't waste time and energy worrying about what you can't control.

'The control test is the most useful thing for me, not stressing about things you can't control. The only things you can control are very limited and lucky for you they are all within your power to influence. In a complex world, I find that very liberating,' said Andrew.

For someone like me, who operated in a state of almost constant chaos and disorganisation (both mental and physical), the idea of a simple test that would cut through the fog of decision making was extraordinarily appealing. The control test was also important because it stopped me from being overly reliant on chance, serendipity, luck, persuasion and hope—and then feeling disappointed when things did not go my way (such disappointment then spoiling my tranquillity).

How could they always go my way if I could, in reality, control so little? In truth, most of my life so far had unfolded in accordance to forces outside my control. There are plenty of goals I've trained my sights on, and worked really hard for—only to fail because forces outside my control (such as timing) intervened. Looking for my first graduate law job in a recession, and receiving only one interview out of a hundred applications is one example that springs to mind. Had I graduated ten years later in a much healthier economy, the outcome would probably have been changed and my life might have gone on a completely different path.

What we can control

According to my interpretation of Stoicism, we can fully control just three things:
1. our character
2. our reactions (and in some cases our actions, but not their outcomes)
3. and how we treat others.

The rest of it is either under our partial control or not up to us at all.

Partial control includes the metaphorical ship's captain who can control the ship but not the weather, while also under our partial control are our bodies and physical appearance. We can control what we put in our body but genetics is really the main determinant of appearance, health and body type—and, with the exception of some advances in science, we have no control over our genetic make-up.

You control much less than you think you do

Control is important to us psychologically because it allows us to feel that we are in the driver's seat, that we are not just drifting, that our lives have a forward momentum, that we have agency and can make choices. We like to think we have a lot of control because it makes us feel safe.

We think we can control certain things: the way the world sees us, our reputation, our opportunities, who we love and who loves us, and how we live. We think we can control our bodies: how they look and function, their shape and size. We think we can control our careers and our prospects, money and security and health. We think we can be the boss of our reputation and shepherd our ascendancy through the world.

Returning to the nautical analogy, we think we are the masters of our ship, in charge of the direction we take. But the conditions—such as storms—are unpredictable and can throw us off course, despite our best intentions, and all our will and effort. The stark and unpalatable truth is we never had that much control to begin with.

Just think about everything in life that is out of your control. You don't control if you are in an accident, if you get sick, whom you meet and fall in love with or who might love you back. You don't control when your parents die or when your friends die or if your children die young or (to an extent) if you have children. You don't control if you get picked for a job or if an investment is fruitful or not. You don't get to decide on your boss or choose your colleagues. You don't have control over whether the person you are dating commits to you, or whether the person you swiped on swipes you back. You don't get a say on when there's an economic collapse or a pandemic or high inflation or a war or an economic collapse or high petrol prices or a rise in interest rates or a shortage of timber from China. You don't get to choose if you lose your job or fall ill, or if you recover from sickness. It's all out of your control. Yet we assume that so much of life is within our control—and that is what causes us problems, angst and unhappiness when things don't go our way.

The notion that we don't control much is terrifying, and can make the world feel unmanageable and chaotic.

We all know people we'd describe as control freaks: helicopter parents; micro-managing bosses; suspicious boyfriends or girlfriends; friends who insist on doing things their way, all the time. But ultimately, according to the Stoics, these people are acting under the illusion of control. It may make *them* feel better to try to control things but they have the same level of ultimate control as everyone else: that is, they can only control their character, their reactions and actions, and how they treat others.

You could argue that your boss has control over you—that is how employment works—but the control is only partial. You could quit, decline to do a task, negotiate, speak to your union or do the task but have freedom of thought about the actual task itself.

Epictetus—who placed the control test so prominently at the centre of his work—was a former slave, as was his mother. He knew all about being controlled, but his master could never completely control him.

Epictetus's thoughts, reactions and character were entirely his own (his actions were not fully in his control).

'There is only one way to happiness and that is to cease worrying about things which are beyond the power of our will,' he said.

Before I started running complicated life situations through the control test, I practised thinking about the test in terms of a game—specifically my favourite game, tennis. While I can control how much I practise, my focus on the game, my general fitness and how much energy I put into the match, ultimately I cannot control whether or not I win. I might have a better opponent or it's raining, and I don't play well in the rain, or I get my period that day and feel like crap. I can just do my best and control the elements that are up to me. But ultimately, winning the game is out of my control.

Then I started thinking about the control test in relation to my work. I could write a column to the best of my ability, but readers or people on social media might hate it, and start barraging me with negative comments, destroying my tranquillity. But their reactions to my work were out of my control. The only thing I could control was doing the column well (my actions), and controlling *my reactions* to their reactions (not to let my tranquillity be disturbed).

Or dating. I could like someone and pursue him, but it was out of my control if he liked me back. I could not control someone else. I could only focus on my own character, how I treated him, and my reactions—particularly if I was being let down or rejected.

Sometimes using the control test leads to unsatisfying outcomes. In 2020, I suffered from tendonitis, an injury around the elbow joint that made it painful to use the computer. The injury itself wasn't in my control but the treatment was. I was advised by a physio to take time off work to rest my arm and reduce my computer use. It was in my control to do that. But the result would have been no income, as I don't get sick leave. Stepping back wasn't an option for me. And so I worked through the injury, maybe to my detriment—but it showed that sometimes applying the control test to the letter has real-life consequences.

Is the control test built for today's world?

Initially, when I looked at Andrew's stick diagram, the Stoic control test seemed almost too simple and too elegant to be a viable tool. These days we are inundated with information and options. Things burn hard and fast online; we're flooded with crisis and information, chaos and the sense (via 24/7 media) that everything that happens is happening *to us*. Does the control test from Epictetus's *Enchiridion* almost 2000 years ago still stand up to this intense moment in history?

In the boardroom I batted these queries and others back to Andrew.

- *Can we control how others act towards us?*
  No, we can only control ourselves, our reactions and the way we treat others.
- *Can we change our loved ones?*
  No, but we can change our reactions to them or how we treat them. (An example—Epictetus said a man should be concerned with his own emotional reaction to his brother's anger, rather than his brother's anger itself.)
- *Can we change a miserable personal circumstance—like being bullied at work?*
  We can change how we act and react.

- *Surely there is greater control when it comes to parenting?*
  We can parent our children to the best of our ability, but ultimately we cannot control how they act, how they turn out or what sort of adults they become.
- *Can we change the people around us who might treat us badly?*
  No, it is only our own character that we have true control over, not the character of others.
- *What about social change?*
  We can effect change through agitating for a systems change or political change—but large systemic change is not in our direct control as an individual.
- *What about big things like war?*
  As individuals living far away, we cannot change wars happening in various parts of the world, but we can control how peaceful we are in our own lives. We can change the way we live, but we cannot change the way those around us live, we can only try to persuade them to do the right thing.

And so back and forth we went . . .

It was true. In every situation we could possibly imagine, we could apply the control test. Without fail, when applying Stoic principles, out came an answer, even if it was not an answer that we wanted, and even if the answer wasn't perfect.

Control in the workplace

Over the course of my Stoic journey, I found some situations where it was harder to apply the control test because I felt entitled to a certain outcome. In those cases, it was hard to come to terms with the fact that I didn't have as much control as I wanted.

It was winter 2020 and Andrew and I were having brunch on Bondi Road. I was in a foul mood as I had just been turned down for a pay rise, despite having written a very compelling letter to my boss about why I should be paid more.

The refusal had totally disrupted my tranquillity. It wasn't just ruining my brunch, it was ruining my whole conception of myself. I had made a judgement that the lack of a pay rise meant that I was not valued by the company. I had been stewing over it for 48 hours now and was getting ever more riled up. Maybe I'd quit! That'd show them!! I'd have no pay, but no pay was better than what I was getting now!

Andrew applied Stoicism to my problem like a doctor prescribing a treatment for a physical ailment.

'It's not worth worrying about. Getting a pay rise isn't within your control,' he reminded me, using Stoicism's first principles. Instead, he said, what was within my control was doing the best job I could and demonstrating to my editors that I was deserving of a pay rise (my actions).

I just had to try my hardest—that's all I could do.

Applying Stoic principles, I could control the way I did my job but the decision to grant me a pay rise was ultimately out of my control. Andrew advised me that if I trained my happiness on something I could control—doing my job well—then I would be happy and tranquil regardless of whether I was more handsomely rewarded for it. Also I was much more likely to get a pay rise if I was performing to the best of my ability. This was not the advice I wanted to hear; after all, I needed the extra money and wanted to feel validation via remuneration. But the advice was very much in keeping with Stoicism's commitment to being clear-eyed and working out my areas of control. Of course I couldn't completely control whether my boss awarded me a pay rise (there may, for example, have been more compelling financial issues for the company to deal with that I was unaware of). But I could try to persuade him by doing the best work possible (which was within my control). I could also try to get another job offer that I could use as leverage, or contact my union. But even when using these tools, getting a pay rise was not in my control—it was for someone else to decide.

Epictetus used the example of a musician performing on stage. The musician can control if they play well or not but cannot control the audience's reaction. 'Take a lyre player: he's relaxed when he performs alone, but put him in front of an audience, and it's a different story, no matter how beautiful his voice or how well he plays the instrument. Why? Because he not only wants to perform well, he wants to be well received—and the latter lies outside his control.'

This is another way of saying that you can only do your best, but you can't actually control the outcome. It was certainly the case with my pay rise.

'FETCH!' CONTROL OF YOUR PET

The control test can also be applied to pet ownership. When you pick up a new puppy, you have a vision of an ideal way for your dog to behave. You can control a certain amount of the dog's behaviour through training and being a good pet owner, but there are certain dogs that, no matter how much you train them, will always poo on the rug when they are stressed, or destroy every shoe you've ever owned when they are a puppy, or bark loudly when someone passes on a skateboard, or get cranky when they haven't been walked. You can take action by training dogs but you do not have complete control over your dog's behaviour, as its actions exist outside your realm of control.

How to cope with lack of control?

Lockdowns during the pandemic were a perfect example where our lack of control was exposed.

How did we cope with a lack of control? For the most part—badly! Rates of drinking, domestic violence and mental illness spiked when people's control over their environment was suddenly subject to extra-ordinary external forces: new laws and policing and the potential to catch a deadly virus, without the protection of a vaccine.

Everywhere since March 2020, I noticed in the collective a feeling of rage, powerlessness and despair connected to this loss of control. It was all over social media; it was in the feral and uncivil way people interacted both online and in public; it was in conversations with my friends.

The lockdown laws were so strict, sudden, heavily policed, financially crippling (for shutdown business, and for individuals who breached the laws and were fined) and many of them seemingly arbitrary and Kafkaesque. People in less wealthy areas in Sydney and Melbourne with a higher number of people from non-English speaking backgrounds faced harsher restrictions, and an increased presence of police on the streets. The feelings of lack of control and autonomy became a default state for pretty much everyone. The new reality came on quickly and was so abrupt, strange and intrusive that it was hard to navigate.

One of the main things the Stoics strived to maintain was their tranquillity—and to not let their equilibrium be disturbed too much by what was outside those few things that they could control.

You are more likely to feel an inner disturbance if you set your heart and mind on something that is *beyond your control* to obtain. There is a conflict then if you want something, but you are not guaranteed to get it. This creates internal tension because you cannot control the outcome—and you risk being upset or disappointed if it doesn't go your way. That tension causes stress, and the outcome could cause unhappiness. The control test is a way of maintaining tranquillity by not worrying about things that are out of your control.

But how to not worry about things outside your control? You just do the control test, and if it's outside of your control then you stop worrying. Simple to say but, as I found out (not just in relation to tendonitis or lockdowns), hard to do.

The control test in a time of law and (health) orders

As 2019 turned into 2020, then 2021, I started applying the control test more systematically and automatically. During the pandemic, the control test really earned its place as a central decision-making tool in my life.

In March 2020, Australia's international borders were closed, effectively ending my hard-won dream career as a travel writer. I had been one of the lucky ones able to make a (partial) living from it for the last ten years, after many years of pitching often unsuccessfully, making contacts, working for very little money, and honing my craft. I had finally broken through and I had enjoyed the privilege of being paid to fly around the world, writing about destinations both exotic and far flung, while often staying in luxurious hotels. It *was* the best job in the world! In 2020, I was set to go to Iran, Europe, the United States and Lebanon. There was and still is absolutely no point dwelling on the loss of these trips, and loss of my travel writing career (would it come back? I didn't know). There was a pandemic on, and there was no way it was safe to travel. What's more, I wasn't allowed to travel. No one was allowed out of Australia without an extreme amount of difficulty and paperwork, for almost two years. Even if I had been allowed out, it would have been extremely hard to return and I would be required to undertake two weeks hotel quarantine at my own expense. (In making these laws, Australian legislators were perhaps unknowingly employing a Stoic maxim from ancient Roman lawmaker Cicero: 'The safety of the people shall be the highest law.')

The control test was easy to apply in relation to my travel-writing job. Did I have control over borders? No. Did I have control over the global collapse of the travel industry? No. Did I have control over the fact that the publications I wrote for were closing down their travel sections and magazines were folding because of a lack of cruise line advertising? No. So I didn't dwell on it, and let it ruin my tranquillity. I just moved on and wrote about other things.

Then there were the internal state border closures. These were actually much more of a headache, because they were so unpredictable. Various borders, in various confusing configurations of states and territories, would open and shut to each other depending on case numbers, virus transmission levels, vaccination rates and new variants. These border closures could happen quickly—and once they closed it was almost impossible to cross them. Funerals, scheduled surgeries, dying relatives, the sale of property—none of it guaranteed an exemption in this era of the *unprecedented*.

I was in Sydney a lot for work, but my home was in country Victoria, a one-hour flight away. I lost count of the number of times I got stuck in one place or the other, a sudden border closure meaning I couldn't get to my home—or I couldn't get to my work in Sydney.

What was I thinking setting up my life in this mad way? Why couldn't I just be like a normal person and live and work in the same place? What was quirky, if workable, before suddenly became unworkable. Could I change the border closures? No. But I could change my reaction to this inconvenience and it was in my control to anticipate that border closures would be an issue until the majority of the population was vaccinated. Using the control test, this then allowed me to establish more of a base in Sydney and rent out country Victoria to friends, so I would not be stuck trying to cross borders. This would improve my tranquillity.

The week I moved back to Sydney more permanently, the city locked down for what would be several months. This was unanticipated. I was taken by surprise (in Westfield Bondi Junction, the day before lockdown—riding the escalator down the shimmering bright mezzanine, the air unnaturally chilled, the strains of muzak hanging in the cold air, and no one there but me and a man with a baby strapped to his chest, frantically scouring the shops for Nespresso coffee pods . . .) but I could not control the lockdown or its timing. During the actual lockdown itself, new laws and health orders frequently changed. I could not control that. Initially we were allowed to go within 10 kilometres of our homes. Police were checking IDs. We could not visit other people's houses and we could not gather in more than groups of ten, then four, then two, then one. I could not control that. When meeting with one other, you had to meet for exercise. (Bondi around this surreal time, in an effort to subvert the lack of control, transformed into one enormous speakeasy, with margarita sellers lining the streets in small takeaway shop fronts, selling powerfully strong drinks in takeaway coffee cups to people pretending to exercise while sipping from the cup and getting quietly blasted on those strange and unseasonably warm winters' nights.)

During this time, within my control was enjoying the 10 kilometres around my apartment and continuing to work from home. I could not control when the 10 kilometres became 5 kilometres (my 5 kilometres ended on the sands of South Bondi, making a swim illegal). Could I do anything about that?

No, I had no control over government health orders. But it was in my control to find beauty spots within my 5-kilometre radius and enjoy those.

Ditto being required to wear a face mask outside. I may not have liked wearing a mask, and I may have found it uncomfortable, but I could control my character—and it showed good character to want others in my community to be safe.

I had to laugh when around this time I read this line from Marcus Aurelius. It was written 2000 years ago—but he could have written it in 2021: 'It stares you in the face. No role is so well suited to philosophy as the one you happen to be in right now.'

During 2020 and 2021, I was applying the control test like crazy, using it more than a dozen times a day as I struggled with new laws, the prospect of being fined and the anger at having my movements curtailed. Taking deep breaths, the control test itself calmed me down. I now had a mechanism to work out what I could and could not control under these entirely strange circumstances, where laws that directly affected the material, practical and emotional aspects of our lives were being enacted and amended on a near-daily basis. The next step after applying the control test was to be okay with rapid change and reality—otherwise I would not find the calm I needed.

Using the control test to cope with change

One of the upsides of following the control test is tranquillity. If you can't control something, then there's no point worrying about it or getting angry. That's just a waste of energy. Instead your energy should be focused on making the most of what you can control.

Modern Stoic philosopher William Irvine wrote in his book *The Stoic Challenge*, 'When the number of options available is limited, it is foolish to fuss and fret. We should instead simply choose the best of them and get on with life. To behave otherwise is a precious waste of time and energy.'

During lockdown, I spoke to an acquaintance, Michelle, who was having a hard time adjusting to changes brought on by the pandemic. This was everyone, right?

In this case, Michelle, a 33-year-old British expat, lived alone in Sydney and worked in marketing. Before the pandemic Michelle had a great life. She casually dated guys whom she met on dating apps, had weekly drinks with her colleagues and played two team sports. On the weekends, she'd travel and go out to restaurants. Her life was great.

But when stay-at-home orders hit Sydney, Michelle fell apart. She could see that her carefully ordered life of regular social contact and group activities would stop altogether and there was nothing left to fill the gap.

Her apartment, which was small, light and close to the city centre suddenly felt like a prison cell where she was confined for 24 hours a day except for the one hour a day she met a friend for a walk.

Michelle very quickly grew despondent about her situation. She was all alone, she told herself—and the feeling soon started corresponding with her reality. She stopped organising walks, and became too depressed to Facetime friends back home. She began lashing out at her boss at work (over Zoom), unconsciously perhaps resenting the job that kept her in a country where she had to experience a friendless lockdown.

After several months, the lockdown lifted but the suffering continued for Michelle. She now harboured a negative view of Australia, believing it was the wrong place for her to live because her lockdown had been so lonely and isolated. And her relationships at work had frayed because she had been angry and unpleasant to her team. She left the country not long after—convinced the whole experience was a folly.

It didn't actually have to be that way for Michelle. Had she applied the control test, Michelle could have made the stressful experience of living alone in a pandemic a richer time. The first step is to acknowledge a change in reality and then to try to adapt. Successful adaptation requires not resisting the change or circumstances as they are, and not looking back and mourning what was—but acknowledging that change is part of life, even change that we do not necessarily like.

Wrote Marcus Aurelius, 'The universe is change; our life is what our thoughts make it.'

To that, Michelle might respond, 'Well that's all well and good to say to accept change but I actually loved my life before. Everything was set up in a way that suited me, and I worked hard to create a life that worked for me. Why should I just be okay about the good things in my life just stopping?'

To which a Stoic would respond: you may not be happy with your new circumstances but the change is outside your control and *what you control is how you respond to change*. Ancient Stoics had to deal with all manner of sudden, often dramatic and unwelcome changes—such as exile to an unfamiliar or unfriendly land at the whim of a powerful enemy. (In many ways stay-at-home orders were like exile, except in reverse.)

Michelle couldn't control the pandemic. She couldn't control the stay-at-home orders. She couldn't control the limits the government set around movement. She couldn't control the opening of shops, bars, cafes and restaurants. So there was a lot outside her control. But she could control her response to these orders. She could control her time in terms of scheduling walks, phone calls and a social bubble with friends. She could control her drinking. She could control (to an extent) how much sleep she got. She could control her exercise regime.

It might have been hard—and it might not have been fun to drag herself out of bed for yet another tedious walk. But using her reason, she would have known that the benefits of doing daily exercise during a stressful period of time outweighed the inertia of staying in bed. (Or as Marcus Aurelius said—in another piece of wisdom that could have been penned in 2021: 'At dawn, when you have trouble getting out of bed, tell yourself: I have to go to work—as a human being. What do I have to complain of, if I'm going to do what I was born for—the things I was brought into the world to do? Or is this what I was created for? To huddle under the blankets and stay warm?' Ha ha ha . . .)

SO HOW DO WE MENTALLY PREPARE FOR CHANGE?

We work out what we can control and can't control about a situation.

Remember: there are only three things in our complete control and these are our character; our reactions and actions; and how we treat others.

If we can't control something, we need to accept it: as an old journalist mentor told me when I asked how to cope with changes in the newsroom, we should learn to 'bend like a reed'. That is, be flexible but grounded.

Maybe we can control *elements* of a situation—like my time in lockdown. Sit down with your journal, summon some rational thought and clarity and look at your situation. Separate the situation into what you can and can't control. Draw a diagram if that helps. The next step— set to work making the most of what you can control and accept what you can't.

We accept what we can't by letting go of resistance. We let go. We stop resisting.

Easier said than done, you might say. But the Stoics, aware of humans' fear of change and resistance to bad times, knew what we needed to get through periods of change and upheaval—and could even thrive under tough circumstances.

Dead time or alive time?

During the pandemic, podcasters and authors Tim Ferriss and Ryan Holiday—both of whom are passionate about Stoicism—outlined a concept called alive time or dead time (Holiday borrowed it from author Robert Greene, who talked about it on one of Holiday's podcasts). That is, stay-at-home orders—whether they be for 3 weeks or, in Melbourne's case, 267 days—are time that can be used one of two ways: in a dead way, where you freak out, get nothing done and spend a lot of your time in passive activities such as watching Netflix, smoking weed or getting angry on social media. Or it can be alive time: a period of time where you grow and utilise the days in a constructive way.

In Sydney's long lockdown of 107 days, I did a bit of both. It started with dead time: a time of freaking out about the virus, not sleeping too well, drinking wine at home as I got spooked about *the numbers*, watching three different news channels one after the other each night, and doom scrolling when I startled awake at 4 a.m. each inky dark, locked-in, groundhog day morning.

Then after a couple of weeks of that, I woke up to the fact that this lockdown could be going for the long haul (this turned out to be correct) and that if I didn't want to get to the end of it a massive mess with a drinking, social media and anger problem then I better turn the ship around.

I thought about what it was that I had wanted to do but had always said I never had the time. There were three things that came to mind, all in different spheres of my life, all within the parameters of the health orders to get done, and all within my control.

The first thing was to improve my skills at tennis. The next was to write another novel. The third was to learn how to drive.

The tennis one I could do. It was within the rules—so I found a coach who could help me unlearn all the bad techniques I had been taught as a kid in the 1980s. Once a week I met him at the nearby courts and was able to afford the lessons because I wasn't going out to restaurants and bars anymore. Increased skills and confidence meant I started scheduling games with friends (also allowed), so a few birds were killed with the one stone: I was exercising, I was socialising and I was improving on a skill.

The novel I also accomplished. I tried to write for an hour every morning and some mornings were better than others. But by the time lockdown ended I had more than 50,000 words, a really decent start on a first draft. One thing I realised about novel writing—which I am sure the ancient Stoics in exile would agree with—is that, no matter what your external circumstances, your imagination is a place of freedom. There is no 5-kilometre limit on where you can roam in your mind. There is no one policing what you think about and write about in the comfort of your own home. While writing can be a slog, I found these mornings on the novel were deliciously sublime. While throughout the rest of my day I felt reality everywhere (police all over my neighbourhood, fining people for sitting down by the fountain to eat a kebab etc.), when I sat down with blank page and a pen, I was free in my mind and my soul to go where I wanted to go. And in doing this for an hour a day, I actually felt more alive than I did for the rest of the day.

The third thing—driving lessons—was also transformative. Here I was, in my forties, still relying on my parents to pick me up from the station every time I went to visit them. It was embarrassing! I was spending thousands of dollars on Ubers! I'd been putting off driving lessons for years because my job as a travel writer meant that I was never in the one place long enough to have consistent lessons or practice. Now I was stuck in one place with the borders shut and I was forbidden to travel. That meant I had enough time to take driving lessons. 'The obstacle in the path becomes the path. Never forget, within every obstacle is an opportunity to improve our condition,' said

Ryan Holiday (who has written a book on the concept, *The Obstacle is the Way*). Or as Marcus Aurelius wrote, 'The mind adapts and converts to its own purposes the obstacle to our acting. The impediment to action advances action. What stands in the way becomes the way.'

In my case, the obstacle (shut borders) had become the way (time to take driving lessons). In using the idea of dead or alive time, I found some of the most negative things about the pandemic actually enabled these positive things to occur.

The art of persuasion

Initially when I was absorbing the control test, I didn't think character, the way you treat other people and my actions and reactions covered a wide area of control. Was our field of influence really so tiny? What of the role of persuasion, where you could try to bring people around to your point of view?

You can try to persuade people—as I did with my email to my boss, asking for a pay rise. Persuasion is important. The art of rhetoric—which was all about persuasion, or presenting compelling arguments—was taught alongside philosophy in ancient times. But ultimately, the outcome of your persuasion is also out of your control. After all, you can't control someone else's mind and thoughts. It's best just to use the control test when assessing your influence over an outcome.

Over time, after applying it in my own life, I came to see the control test as a practical, efficient and elegant technique to sort out the things over which I should and shouldn't worry about, and the things I can change versus the things I have no power over. I'd write down the problem—say it was applying for a rental that I had my heart set on—and then apply the control test to the situation.

No—I did not have control as to whether I would be successful in getting the rental apartment I desired. Okay, cool, good to know.

Said Epictetus: 'We should always be asking ourselves: "Is this something that is, or is not, in my control?"'

When I was unsuccessful in getting the apartment, it didn't perturb me as much as it once would have, because I had already assessed that the situation was outside my control, and had rehearsed getting rejected in a fleeting form of negative visualisation.

Now I try to apply Epictetus's principles every time I have an irritation, annoyance, problem, desire, need, want, goal or disturbance. It doesn't always come easily. I have to consciously apply the control test. Sometimes doing so feels laborious. But working out what is and isn't within my control early on can save me a lot of angst down the road.

I try to return to the control test several times a day and find it calming to have a bedrock, a rule that I can consult no matter what the situation. Is this in my control? I might have been unsuccessful in my application for an apartment, which makes me feel unhappy, which might then ruin my tranquillity. Let's bring in the control test. Getting the apartment is not within my full control, but my reaction is in my control. I can choose to stay cool and not react. Or I can react and escalate the negative emotions.

What about the bigger things?

Huge life events—like falling in love with someone—can also be subject to the control test. You can't control someone into loving you, and it is out of your control if they want a relationship with you. The same applies if you are in a relationship and one person wants to break up. The control test is a valuable tool in learning to let go and move on. Of course, it's never that easy in the moment. Love and loss are not neat feelings that can be summarily dealt with—but we'll talk more about that later in the chapter, 'How to be Untroubled'.

The climate

For structural problems like climate change or inequality, the control test enables me to work out what part I can play (fly less, for a start)— and where I should be holding the government to account or voting in climate-focused independents. The government of the day has control over policies to mitigate some of the worst problems in our society, and the democratic process enables us to play a part in creating the type of society we would like to live in.

When fires filled the city skies with ash in late 2019, and I stood on a lawn at the water's edge at a product launch, sipping a newly released sooty rosé, there mightn't have seemed much I could have done about the filthy air. But in relation to climate collapse, this is what I can control:

- talking to friends and experts—and acting on good advice and sound science
- taking part in community and grass-roots action groups
- voting
- becoming informed
- using reason and rationality, and avoiding fake news
- planting trees
- divesting from fossil fuels in my investments including superannuation
- and developing my own sustainability practices, such as flying less and taking public transport.

Doing the thing well

The Stoics were not ones to just sit on their hands and say, 'Oh well, no point trying because it's out of my control.' Instead you should do everything to the best of your ability (which is actually something you do have control over) but realise that you cannot control the outcome. As a result, your energy is put into doing the best you can do, and not in fretting about whether the outcome is successful.

Used well, the control test will change how you use your energy and where you place your care and attention. Your energy should be focused on the first part of the equation: *doing the thing well.* And you should not direct any energy or worry to things out of your control, such as *the outcome or people's response to what you do*, because that is wasted energy. You will only end up with your tranquillity disturbed.

Working out what I could and couldn't control was empowering. I just stopped (or tried to stop) worrying about things outside my control, which allowed me to be clear-eyed, not deluded and see situations for what they were. I got so much of my energy and tranquillity back when I stopped living in a fantasyland, where I believed I had more control than I really did. I also became less frustrated with life when things didn't go my way.

Preparation is within your control

As for my own organisational chaos, the control test has been a life changer in giving me some clarity in what I can and cannot change. It has also helped me prepare better, because controlling preparation is within my control. And preparation can lead to a better outcome—whether that be a smoother trip to the airport (by packing the night before) or a better meeting with my boss (by preparing notes and talking points). I've seen one of my collaborators, Benjamin Law, write out lines of dialogue to say before he goes into a tricky (telephone) meeting, so he can stick to the point, not get taken off track by whomever he is speaking to, and achieve a clear aim in the meeting. Not being able to control an outcome doesn't mean you shouldn't prepare.

Preparation doesn't always mitigate unfortunate things happening. I still lose laptops, important work on my computer, phones, keys and diaries—but, once something is gone and I have done all I can to retrieve it, then I move on if I cannot get it back.

Cope with disaster

'If he lose a hand through disease or war, or if some accident puts out one or both of his eyes, he will be satisfied with what is left, taking as much pleasure in his impaired and maimed body as he took when it was sound. But while he does not pine for these parts if they are missing, he prefers not to lose them.'

—**Seneca**

'If you want to improve, reject such reasonings as these: "If I neglect my affairs, I'll have no income; if I don't correct my servant, he will be bad." For it is better to die with hunger, exempt from grief and fear, than to live in affluence with perturbation; and it is better your servant should be bad, than you unhappy.'

—**Epictetus**

From mid-March 2020, when all the offices shut and workers were sent home, Andrew and I started taking our Stoicism sessions outside, on foot. In a nice piece of serendipity, both of us had moved within a block of each other in the beachside suburb of Tamarama. I'd walk to the end of my street, turn a corner, descend the steep stairs in an overgrown gully, past the bursts of colour from the flame trees, and meet Andrew on the stairs at the gate of his house. From there, we'd walk down to the beach and veer either left or right, depending on what was the sunnier side of the cliffs. Sometimes we'd stop for a coffee or some food, or if the weather was good, we'd have a swim.

Going for walks suited a discussion of Stoicism. Ideas could be batted back and forth, and the pace of debate settled into a sort of ambulatory rhythm. Walking alongside one another we could discuss problems we were having and how to apply Stoicism to them, or have a disagreement without the intensity of eye contact that comes from sitting across a table, leading sometimes to difficult or awkward topics being skated over. Walking alongside someone, while trying to process lessons about dying or getting sick or losing work, seemed a bit easier while looking straight ahead to the blue horizon.

During these walks, a dynamic had become established where I played the sceptic to Andrew's straight man, Lucilius to his Seneca. Each new principle we explored would come under a barrage of doubt and questioning from me. Andrew, who was naturally more of a Stoic than me, defended the principles and highlighted how they worked in real life. I counter-argued some points, and kept an open mind on others. Then I went away, read some more, and tried to see if any of the theory could be applied successfully to my life.

Andrew and I were coincidently or perhaps unconsciously mimicking what the Roman Stoics saw as being the ideal way to learn philosophy—and that is through dialogue and friendship. Modern philosopher Martha Nussbaum wrote in *The Therapy of Desire*: 'The paradigm of philosophical interaction is the quiet conversation of friends who have an intimate knowledge of one another's character and situation.'

In *Moral Letters to Lucilius*, Seneca wrote that conversation is 'more useful' than writing, 'even intimate letter writing', 'because it creeps bit by bit into the soul'.

Compared with personal conversation, 'lectures prepared in advance and poured out to a listening crowd have more volume but less intimacy. Philosophy is good practical advice; nobody gives advice in a loud voice.'

But the conversation on our walks was more than a passive thera-peutic application of Stoic principles, more than just *'good practical advice'*; it was also an interrogation of Stoicism by two people with different temperaments, intellectual skill sets and life circumstances. One intention of these conversations was not just to see if the principles worked in our personal lives, but also to drag the philosophy into the 2020s and hold it to the light to see where the flaws or poor joins were. Stoicism for example didn't really fit well with discussion around intersectionality. Nor did it seem to accord with current norms and discussion regarding, for example, disability and health or structural inequality. And both of us struggled to see how action that led to social justice and societal change could fit in neatly with the control test.

This disconnection with today's norms was definitely the case with *preferred indifferents*—where Stoics believed character, virtue and rational thinking were things that you should go out of your way to nurture and protect, while things going wrong with your body or being thrust into poverty were a preferred indifferent (that is, it's pref-erable to have health and wealth than not but ultimately you should be indifferent).

But first—what is the doctrine of preferred indifferents?

76

The Stoics classified a range of things including wealth, health and reputation as a 'preferred indifferent'—meaning it's preferable to have them but you should essentially be indifferent as to whether you've got them or not. That means not clinging to things or falling apart if you lose them.

Instead, your character is the most important thing. Are you behaving well or badly? Are you cultivating the things that the Stoics called 'the virtues': justice, moderation, wisdom and courage? Are you relaxed? Is your inner self tranquil? Do you treat others well? Are you able to control your anger? These things were more important than the accumulation of reputation and capital. They are even more important than your health.

For the Stoics, it's wrong to consider wealth as a virtue, when you can use your money badly—say, to buy a lot of drugs, or weapons that may later kill someone, or products that are harmful to the environment. But nor is money a vice, as you can use it well—to give it to charity or create jobs for others. Because the use of money varies, Stoic philosophers labelled it an 'indifferent'. That means you shouldn't care whether you have it or not, unlike the Cynic philosopher Diogenes (c. 404 BC) who believed that wealth corrupted those who had it and so was therefore a negative—but more on him later.

The early Stoics realised that there were degrees of indifference. It is completely natural to want to have enough food to eat, to live in a warm, comfortable house, to be able to socialise and be part of a community. Therefore the wealth that allowed you to do all these things was preferable to not being able to afford them. This category of things evolved to become known as preferred indifferents—and was expanded to include life, health, pleasure, beauty, strength, wealth, good reputation and noble birth.

As long as these things didn't get in the way of achieving virtue, then you could have some nice things. In fact some of the Roman Stoics, such as Seneca and Marcus Aurelius, were extremely wealthy. (And many of the modern-day adherents to Stoicism who can be found in Silicon Valley are also extremely wealthy.) So while it's fine to be wealthy, you just have to be *okay* with (or indifferent to) losing all your wealth.

The dispreferred indifferents (the things that you don't really want but generally should be indifferent to) included death, disease, pain, ugliness, weakness, poverty, low repute and ignoble birth.

The keyword here is 'indifferent'. Marcus Aurelius in *Meditations* said we should be 'indifferent towards indifferent things'. So even though it's preferable to have money, a good reputation, your health and a nice home, you should remain indifferent to whether you gain them or lose them. That is, you should be *okay* with having them—and okay with not having them.

The reason for cultivating indifference is important: each of these things (health, wealth and reputation) is outside your control. Without any fault or action of your own, you could lose your reputation, then your job, then your money, your house and maybe your marriage. You'll almost certainly lose your looks as you age. If you live long enough, you might lose mobility, cognitive ability and other aspects of your health.

In order to avoid being too pained by the loss of such things (losses that can come on suddenly, losses that, as you get older, seem to stack up and up), it's far better to have been indifferent to them in the first place. It's a way of building your inner fortitude and strength for when a crisis comes.

Naturally, for a Stoic, this indifference extends indifference to life and death, because you have no control over when you die, and in fact the one certainty you have in life is that you *will* die.

Old mate Diogenes

In order to explain to you why, for Stoics, losing these external things essentially DOES NOT MATTER, I need to introduce you to one of the most intriguing characters from the ancient world: Diogenes.

Born around 404 BC in what became modern-day Turkey, Diogenes was a philosopher who founded the Cynic school of philosophy.

Just like the word 'stoicism' got a bad linguistic massage over the ages to mean something quite distinct from what the philosophy stands for, so too with Cynic philosophy. The Cynics were not distrustful and hardened in the way that modern usage of 'cynic' suggests; instead they were questioning, highly unconventional and strived to live as closely as possible to nature. As a result they were extremely unmaterialistic and wonderfully weird.

The most famous Cynic was Diogenes, whom we still talk about today because of his extreme audaciousness. He basically gave no fucks.

Some of the main things to know about Diogenes are that he lived in a barrel (probably an old wine barrel), masturbated in public and was big into disruption.

An extreme ascetic, Diogenes made it his life's goal to challenge established customs and values. He argued that we are too governed by customs and culture—and do not investigate the true nature of things. In the Athenian marketplace, he carried around a lamp in the daytime claiming to be looking for an honest man. He attended public lectures but distracted other attendees by bringing in food and drink.

When he saw a peasant child drinking water from his hands by a stream, Diogenes threw away his cup and, impressed, said, 'Fool that I am, to have been carrying superfluous baggage all this time!'

Diogenes's simple values and lack of material possessions were meant to show that we waste our lives working and striving for things that are not necessary or meaningful for life. By living his philosophy, Diogenes proved that you need nothing material—not even a cup—to have a good life. If you owned nothing and wanted nothing, then you have taken your power back, because you are not trying to get anything from anybody. You are entirely self-reliant. You are crisis proof—because anything going wrong externally, such as your house being destroyed, is not a crisis to you.

The Stoics agreed with some of the ideas of Diogenes and the Cynics but diverged when it came to money. The Cynics rejected convention and anything they saw as not being basic and from nature, whereas the Stoic view of nature was enlarged to include things made by humans such as laws, institutions and economies.

Don't be injured twice

Why should we see things that are highly prized in our society as a preferred indifferent? In part to suffer less (we saw this in the chapter 'How to Work Out What Matters' when not worrying about what you can't control means you suffer less when your circumstances change). The adoption of the concept of 'preferred indifferents' acts as a protective mechanism. The Stoics often talked about not being injured twice. Take the example of losing your job. The first injury is losing the thing itself (i.e. losing your job and the salary and prestige that comes with it) but the second injury is getting upset about your job and losing your tranquillity. Sometimes the second injury—the one you inflict on yourself through anguish at the loss—is a lot more difficult to overcome than the first. A typical by-product of the second, self-inflicted injury is sadness, depression, bitterness or a lust for revenge. You might be angry at your boss, or bitter at your co-workers for continuing to be employed, or resentful at your spouse who is starting to worry about money and urging you to take the first job that comes along. All these knock-on effects are second injuries arising from the first (the loss of your job). This second loss is also entirely avoidable and often just hurts you further. As St Augustine said, 'Resentment is like drinking poison and waiting for the other person to die.'

If you didn't feel the loss of the first thing so keenly, because you genuinely saw it as a preferred indifferent, then the following problems wouldn't flow on. You would naturally be sad about the loss of your job and subsequent income, but you would work hard to harbour no ill feeling and you would strive to maintain inner tranquillity in the face of the setback. That way you recover from the first setback a lot more quickly.

The preferred indifferents made sense theoretically. As Andrew and I went back and forth debating them, I admitted that I could see the logic of health and wealth as a preferred indifferent. After all, both things come and go randomly—'You could get hit by a bus while crossing the road!' I kept on remarking as we crossed roads—regardless of how much we think we could control them. Viewing these things as preferred indifferents would certainly help insure against suffering when things go wrong.

But I also wondered, even with the best preparations in the world, were humans really built to be indifferent to suffering. Could we really train ourselves to expect the worst, and then just be *chill* when the worst happened? And wasn't it natural to want nice things—like a lovely home, to be respected by our peers, or cherish a healthy body—and then be devastated if those things were lost?

Imagining the worst

I returned home from the walk (careful not to get hit by a passing car) and did some negative visualisation exercises about how would I respond if I lost all my money, my home was repossessed by the bank, my reputation got dragged through the mud, I was cancelled on social media, I got taken to court, I lost my column at *The Guardian*, my TV show never got made, members of my family got sick and then I got diagnosed with a serious illness. I thought about my Tamarama house burning down after one of my hippie housemates left a bundle of sage smouldering in the hall. I thought about my laptop melting in the fire and destroying all my work that I hadn't backed up in the Cloud. I'm not going to lie:, it was a massive downer of an exercise.

I couldn't imagine being sanguine about any of *that*. What I could imagine was that, if I lost my money and reputation, it was more likely I'd become bitter and angry, vowing revenge on those who had brought me down. Or maybe I would throw myself headlong into hard work and high-risk schemes, plotting and dreaming of getting it all back, regaining my reputation and my pride—and not being satisfied until I did.

A lot of this is human nature, combined with the values of our age (money, status, brands, and so on). Every day in the media there are stories about people investing enormous chunks of time and capital into protecting the preferred indifferents in their lives. People spend years in court bringing defamation actions to correct their reputation, or they commit high-risk financial crimes so they can live a luxurious lifestyle. They gamble it all to hang onto an indifferent.

As for health, if I got sick, maybe I would vow not to stop treatments or look for a cure until I was well again. Maybe I would become depressed at my limitations. But Stoicism challenged me not to.

Another sunny winter day, another walk—this one towards Clovelly that took us across a cemetery overlooking the Pacific Ocean. The *memento mori* was so obvious and literal that it was like a scene, stage-designed by some imaginary Stoic god. There lay the bodies returned to the earth, nothing but dust in a box. There are the chiselled dates in marble—the date of birth and the date of death—all of a life represented by the dash in between.

How many of those people buried on the hill thought they were immortal? How many spent their lives chasing a preferred indifferent? How many lived fully and with purpose in the dash between the years? And yet how easy was it for us to drift, alive and drinking our takeaway coffees, on a sunny winter's day among the dead and not to have the shadow fall: that one day this will be each of us in the ground (or if you so choose, one day you will be ash scattered off those cliffs).

Before these walks I would think about the things I wanted to discuss—maybe an issue that was going on for me that week and I wanted to run through a Stoic lens, or a concept I'd read about that I wanted to explore further or get Andrew's take on. But this time I was keen to return to the preferred indifferents. On these coastal walks with Andrew, I would throw all these worst-case scenarios at him.

We'd be sitting close to the edge of the cliffs and I'd say, 'Okay, what if a gust of wind came along, knocked me off the cliff and I broke my spine?'

Or once when I got sunscreen in my eyes, temporarily blinding me—and I was off the path and near the water and the wind was up and I said, not unreasonably, 'What about now, if I was swept off the cliff's edge because I can't see anything?'

Or 'You are wrongly accused of a crime and spend time in gaol, your reputation is ruined. Are you indifferent?'

Or 'You make a bad business decision and have to sell your house—and move back in with your parents. You okay with that?'

Andrew told me how he was okay with losing things classified as a preferred indifferent. 'I lived in a tiny room in a share house in London. I could go back to living in that small room if I had to.'

He said that unconsciously he had been practising the preferred indifferents since he was a child. Instead of bringing a chocolate treat, like a Mars Bar, to school to eat at recess, and have that treat stolen by a more aggressive child, he just never had a Mars Bar. Better to never have it than endure the upset of having it stolen, was his reasoning. Now as an adult, Andrew said he made sure he was able to enjoy inexpensive wine, so he didn't get a palate for expensive wine. His reasoning—a sophisticated palate is likely to be frustrated if he lacked the means to satisfy it with expensive wines.

'With expensive things, you don't eschew them but you don't get used to them—you enjoy them as a bonus in your life,' he told me.

As for food, 'If you have a beautiful dinner—live it up—but be prepared to return to porridge the next day.'

The return to porridge that Andrew referred to, or drinking average wine, is an echo of an old Stoic technique found in Seneca's *Moral Letters to Lucilius*: that is, to practise periodic poverty as a way of habituating yourself to a different, less opulent lifestyle.

'Is this the condition I feared?'

Seneca advised his friend Lucilius:

[to] set aside a certain number of days, during which you shall be content with the scantiest and cheapest fare, with coarse and rough dress, saying to yourself the while: 'Is this the condition that I feared?' It is precisely in times of immunity from care that the soul should toughen itself beforehand for occasions of greater stress . . . Let the pallet be a real one, and the coarse cloak; let the bread be hard and grimy. Endure all this for three or four days at a time, sometimes for more, so that it may be a test of yourself instead of a mere hobby. Then, I assure you, my dear Lucilius, you will leap for joy when filled with a pennyworth of food, and you will understand that a man's peace of mind does not depend upon Fortune; for, even when angry she grants enough for our needs.

Tim Ferriss follows Seneca's advice. Ferriss said, 'I will regularly, three continuous days per month minimum, practise fasting. I will do that from early Thursday dinner to an early Sunday dinner to simply expose myself to the sensation of real hunger.'

Other people he knows go further. One of Ferriss's friends—a 'very successful CEO and author'—schedules a week every four months 'when he will effectively camp out in his living room, in a sleeping bag, and he will survive on cheap instant coffee and instant oatmeal (perhaps at a cost of 15 dollars per week maximum)'.

He does this so 'he can make do and in fact, often thrive with next to nothing'.

The CEO realises that if he misses out on a deal or has some losses, he can deal with the outcome better because of thriving under tougher conditions.

(Although a caveat for these experiments is how different the experience of poverty is when it is involuntary, and how when you undertake a Stoic practice, like the ones described above, psychologically you are aware that the difficult experience has an end date and you will be returning to a comfortable lifestyle.)

Said Ferriss, 'Perhaps unexpectedly at the end of such an experiment, people will very often be in a better mental state, feel more content than they did beforehand. It's very freeing.'

A couple of years ago I went on an extreme fast. I hadn't started my Stoic journey back then but it did give me a big taste of the deprivation that Seneca (and Tim Ferriss—and also Andrew—talk about).

For two weeks I ate no food, just drank foul-tasting Chinese herbs (imagine the taste of old cigarette butts floating in brackish creek water), then for the following three weeks I ate only small amounts of cucumber and poached chicken. I fasted because I was writing about the experience for a magazine, after Australia's then prime minister Malcolm Turnbull lost a lot of weight on the regime.

Turnbull is not the only politician to embark on a radical or restrictive diet. Many politicians including Anthony Albanese, Bill Shorten and Josh Frydenberg have lost weight before an election campaign to prove to voters that if they can discipline themselves around food, then they have a disciplined enough character to lead the nation. They are perhaps unconsciously trying to exhibit the Stoic virtue of 'temperance'.

I was not leading the nation, but I had never been on a diet before and I was curious as to whether I could carry such a restrictive regime through to the end. I ate so little that I lost 14 kilograms (which I put back on over the following two years). During the fast I mostly slept, felt weak, had vivid and frightening dreams, smelt bad, craved food, had no energy, suffered intense headaches and scary heart palpitations.

But the whole experience was also an exercise in surviving on next to nothing.

In the months after the fast, my relationship with food changed dramatically. When I started eating again, I was full after one bean and a tiny piece of fish. It was delicious. I was sated. I did not need any more food. I thought back to all the times when I needed a snack after two or three hours, all the times I felt unable to concentrate and got angry if I even missed one meal! At the time, my doctor said that, although he did not advocate extreme fasts, he thought short periods of fasting were good to practise occasionally, as they gave us a taste (so to speak) of what it was like to survive on very little food, or have food insecurity. 'We have abundance, while much of the world doesn't have enough,' he told me.

Like the Stoics practising fasting, experiencing prolonged hunger and discomfort gave me the confidence to know that if I needed to, I could go a lot longer than I had once thought without eating.

Tim Ferriss said:

Practising poverty or rehearsing your worst-case scenario in real life, not just journaling, not just in your head, I find very, very important. Certainly I expose myself to a lot of duress and pain in, say, the form of ice baths and cold exposure simply to develop my tolerance for the then unavoidable pain and disruption that comes to all of us. The more you schedule and practice discomfort deliberately, the less unplanned discomfort will throw off your life and control your life.'

Wear weird clothes—create a shame vaccine

Another form of this exercise in deliberately making things harder for yourself, was something eccentric that Cato (95 BC) practised. Cato was a powerful Roman senator, who led the opposition to Julius Caesar in the last years of the Roman Republic. He was taught Stoic philosophy while he was young and wore tunics of unpopular colours and would walk around barefoot.

According to Plutarch:

When he [Cato] saw that a purple which was excessively red and vivid was much in vogue, he himself would wear out the dark shade. Again, he would often go out into the streets after breakfast without shoes or tunic. He was not hunting for notoriety by this strange practice, but accustoming himself to be ashamed only of what was really shameful, and to ignore men's low opinion of other things.

This was a way of Cato training himself to see reputation and status as a preferred indifferent and to be ashamed of only those things truly worth being ashamed of. And for a Stoic, the only true thing to be ashamed of is if your character is faulty. (Cato thought character was of such importance that he killed himself in extremely grisly fashion—self-disembowelment—rather than live under a corrupt ruler.)

I have practised my own form of sartorial shame vaccine whenever I don a piece of clothing I call the Big Puffer (see box).

THE BIG PUFFER

The Big Puffer was a gift—one that has caused as much amusement as it has kept me warm. One day my youngest brother Matt arrived at my place in the country, in the middle of a very cold winter, with a jacket he had found in a charity shop.

'The thing with this jacket,' said my brother in his most serious voice, 'is that you cannot wear it outside the house'.

'Why not? That would defeat the whole purpose of a jacket. A jacket is something that you wear when you go outside.'

I pulled the jacket from its cover. It sort of bounced out. I could see why he advised me not to wear it in public. It wasn't a normal puffer jacket.

It was a gigantic puffer that resembled a sleeping bag with arms. To call it bulky was an understatement. It looked like an inflated life raft and sat on the kitchen floor taking up an enormous amount of space.

I put the jacket on and we both cracked up laughing. My brother punched me in the arm and I didn't feel a thing.

The next morning I disobeyed my brother and wore the jacket outside, to the farmers' market. Walking in it was difficult. I could not swing my arms. They sort of sat away from my body at 45-degree angles—suspended by great volumes of nylon and goose down. But slowly crossing the highway, I felt invincible—as if the bulk of the jacket would protect me if I was hit by a car.

'I can't believe you wore that outside,' said my brother with disgust when I got home. I was wearing the hilarious puffer—but really, like

Cato I was 'accustoming myself to be ashamed only of what was really shameful'.

That night it was very cold—bitter in fact—and I decided to wear the puffer out to a documentary film festival. There were many other people wearing puffers at the film festival but they were the Uniqlo sort that are streamlined and flat. They were flattering puffers.

When I ran into friends at the theatre they immediately started laughing and then hitting me on either side of my body and saying, 'It's Gore-Tex' over and over. This was apparently a Seinfeld reference to the episode where George wore a similar big puffer to Jerry's, and Jerry and Elaine mocked him and whacked him in the arms.

After the film, people took pictures of me in the jacket and the theatre owner made me into a meme and put me on their Facebook page next to a picture of George Costanza in his big puffer saying: 'It's Gore-Tex!'

I took the big puffer to southern Turkey. It was winter and snowing heavily. I was warm but I got laughed at in the street there too. People took photos. Dogs tried to hump me. Something about the puffer made me sexually attractive to animals. I sweated in the snow, even though the temperature was minus 10. The big puffer had transcended cultural, language and even species barriers. Despite its bulk, whenever I wore it, it lightened the mood.

When I wear it now, not only am I warm, but I also feel Stoic. I may look like a dickhead, but I feel a tiny bit like Cato.

First World problems

It helps to think of these exercises (the short-term fasting, the silly clothes) as a kind of vaccine or inoculation against changes in fortune. After all, how many of us fall apart at the slightest hint of hardship, shame, embarrassment or failure? Remember when you last missed a meal, made a joke that didn't land, forgot somebody's name, or had a holiday cancelled, or when you had to deal with no wi-fi or you ran out of coffee and had to have the powdered version, or a thread pulled on your new jumper, or your nice clothes that you planned to wear to the party were not ready at the drycleaners? All these First World problems, all these small, annoying discomforts, can destroy our tranquillity or—even worse—ignite anger, then have a knock-on effect on other areas of our life.

But if you habituate yourself to small hardships—such as a few days of fasting or going barefoot or being deliberately cold or looking stupid in public—when the real problems come along you will have these advantages:

* you have had some experience with hardship
* you know you can handle hardship
* you realise it's not the end of the world—and that your character is really the only thing that matters.

Health—the hardest lesson

But what about our health? Surely it's more difficult to inoculate ourselves against the loss of good health, mobility, energy and vitality?

As health is not in our complete control and not vital for the cultivation of virtue, the Stoics categorised it as a preferred indifferent. The Stoics said as long as our character is intact, then the health of our bodies is secondary. I have to admit this is a big call. But you'll remember Epictetus had the use of only one leg. Our health is beyond the power of our will. How often have we been sick, and willed ourselves to recover quickly, but instead had to let the illness take its own course?

Instead, the Stoics say think of everything you have (including your health) as not your own, but simply on loan, that one day will be taken back. Then when it is taken, you will not be surprised, you will not be bitter and your tranquillity will not be disturbed.

Once again, I had the opportunity to put that to the Stoic test.

I was already a few years into my Stoic journey when my health took a battering. I had already spent a couple of years negatively visualising being ill or infirm. Then came the inevitable time to put it into practice.

In November 2021 I agreed to be a guest judge on a reality TV show and between moving between locations I concussed myself climbing into a troop carrier. Hoisting myself into the back of the vehicle with too much energy, I shot into the roof at great velocity.

'Oof,' said everyone in the back of the troopie as I hit the roof.

'Yeah, yeah, I'm okay,' I said. After half an hour with a plastic bag of ice on my head that was leaking over my face in what looked like a grotesque parody of tears, I thought I had recovered, and carried on as usual.

But that night back in Sydney I started feeling off. At Una's restaurant—carving through their schnitzel the size of a placemat—I had a sudden urge to vomit. My head didn't feel right. I had to go home immediately.

The next day was woozy and slow. After being given the all-clear by doctors in the emergency room (I had a concussion, it would heal in its own time), I flew back to Victoria. I even attended a gig. But all was not well.

By the time I got to my parents' house I needed to rest.

After picking me up from the station, my parents looked aghast, not delighted, when they saw me.

'Your eye wasn't just bloodshot, it had blood in it. And your complexion was grey—like cement,' observed my mother a week later. 'We were worried about you.'

Soon after arriving at their house, I took to the bed in the downstairs guest room, where I stayed for a week and emerged only for meals.

My parents were impressed at the amount I was sleeping. 'It's like you're in an induced coma,' said my mother.

In a way, I was. I couldn't stay awake for more than a few hours at a time. As I spent long hours down there in a hectic, vast dreamscape, I hoped that I was healing.

In my week of deep rest, whole days passed where nothing happened. I could scarcely register them as 'days' as they merged in with the nights, and then into the following mornings. Without anything to do or anywhere to be, I could just follow the pull of sleep back down to the timeless place.

My waking life was also featureless. Concussed, I couldn't handle stimulation, confusion or too much information. I found looking at the fall of tweets down my phone too much. News on the internet, particularly live blogs, was also too overwhelming. Another hourly, daily addiction just gone. My brain just wanted white walls, silence, dreams.

Executive functioning was also shot. The day after I got concussed, I purchased three tickets to the wrong destinations or the wrong dates while booking flights back to Melbourne. I just couldn't focus.

One of the worst things I experienced was an almost continuous sense of panic that I was destined to be forever brain impaired and low on energy. When you are in the middle of sickness or are injured, particularly with something that shows no immediate signs of improving, it can be easy to think that you will never get better.

The loss of health—even temporarily—is a massive blow. And having experienced it and freaked out that I would be living in my parents' guest bedroom . . . forever . . . (and forever sleeping), I wondered rather hazily, how we could be *indifferent* if we get sick or injured.

But I was also beginning to understand the Stoic approach. Like money, and reputation, we should cultivate indifference because our health is not entirely within our control. If a different region of the brain had been struck, I might *still* be lying in my parent's guest bedroom, shades drawn at midday.

It's luck. But my weeks of being injured made me think like a Stoic when it came to my recovery. I negatively visualised not getting better, while working out what in my environment I could control (not being overly stimulated, not going on the internet, sleeping as much as possible) and trying to recover.

Resilience

While aspects of human behaviour never change, society in the 2020s is very different from life in the pre-Christian era. Now we need— and should demand—resilience on two fronts. We need internal or personal resilience to handle life's storms including loss of health, income, reputation and relationships. But we are also in a position where we should demand resilient systems of government. Robust systems provide a safety net to those struggling—and with both external and internal resilience, individuals and the community are best able to weather destabilising events.

An example of this is a strong health and hospital system supported by the government and paid for by taxes—and open to all. You may lose the use of your leg and have to personally cope with the loss, but the loss compounds without hospitals, funding for rehabilitation and support with good services. It is not within the framework of Stoicism to have a government that discards the needs of the poorest and most vulnerable citizens. Stoicism is not a survival-of-the-fittest philosophy as imagined by some libertarians. Instead, a model of a resilient government and governmental systems that support a resilient populace is very much in keeping with Stoic principles and their conception of community, interdependence and the virtue of justice.

Health and the control test

We have only partial control over our health. We could step out onto the road and get hit by a bus, or get electrocuted by plugging in a faulty lamp or hit our heads and become concussed while getting into a troop carrier. Our fragile bodies are vulnerable to countless injuries and illness.

And we all know someone who was either vegan or teetotal or went to CrossFit every day or cycled everywhere . . . In short, they did everything right—and they still got sick and died. Meanwhile your 90-year-old neighbour still smokes and drinks and has never had a sick day in his life.

So by classifying health as a preferred indifferent, and realising it is out of our control, we are not going to disrupt our tranquillity too much if we have negative health outcomes. We can work hard to be healthy and to give ourselves the best chance of having a healthy body. But the ultimate outcome is not entirely up to us.

The Stoics did not intend this to be a licence to be passive and eat all the junk food or neglect our bodies. The Stoic virtue of temperance applies very much to our bodies as much as to our emotions.

While I recovered from my head injury over time and now would say that I am completely recovered, I leaned on Stoicism a lot when I thought that maybe I would not get better. I tried to keep calm. And I reminded myself that at least my character was not harmed in the injury. Although I might be tired or else asleep for a lot of the time, at least I was still able to practise the Stoic virtues of courage, justice, temperance and wisdom. The head injury had not affected these things. In fact the four virtues were more important than ever in getting me through that hard time.

We have it all around the wrong way

Our society does not support the cultivation of indifference to our health, reputation or financial position. In fact, the opposite is the case; we orient our whole lives not just to create these towers (towers of health, wealth and status) but to fiercely protect them. We build our whole life around these things and to lose them in one sense is to lose our life's work.

But Stoicism says our life's work is in honing the four virtues, our character, and how we treat others. Material possessions, health and our status will come and go, ebb and flow, often shifting through outside forces that we can't control.

The lesson of preferred indifferents is one of the most difficult but powerful lessons of Stoicism. Like a lot of Stoicism, it is both elegant and complex, simple and incredibly tough.

It's not unusual over the course of a lifetime to act well and prudently but suffer due to the normal ups and downs that occur for every person, in every lifetime. The journey is bumpy for everyone.

Any of us could be just one more lockdown, fire or flood away from closing the doors of our small business for good. Or one crazy rumour away from a fatal blow to our reputation. Or one freak accident away from good health. Or one loose email sent to the wrong person away from losing our job. These things happen to everyone, at some point, often when we least expect it. And the Stoics protected themselves from some of the shocks of such events by seeing the things outside their control as preferred indifferents.

How does this indifference look? It looks like holding the reins lightly. It means not clinging too tightly to money, reputation and (if you are lucky) your good looks but being pleased when you have them, and absolutely comfortable with losing them. It also means practising negative visualisation—imagining losing it all and starting from scratch.

You can also practise the preferred indifferents using tips from Seneca, Cato and Tim Ferriss and conduct experiments into fasting or being mocked or making yourself uncomfortable. You can swim in a cold lake in winter or dress in a woollen jumper at the height of summer. You can fast for several days or, as Seneca recommends, temporarily narrow your diet down to something simple like vegetable soup and 'hard bread'. Or you can do as my friend Andrew does— and not develop a taste or a habit for fine, expensive things and experiences lest you lose the means of affording them.

Or you can do what I did when I had a head injury: I took it as a taste of what was to come or what could be if I suddenly became permanently incapacitated. It was also a lesson in the randomness of events. One minute you are getting into a vehicle too fast, the next you are wanting to vomit at an Austrian restaurant and going to the emergency room.

You can do what I and many others do—and that is detach from your devices periodically and retreat either by yourself or with others to the countryside and have several days of contemplation, plain food, meditation and journalling, away from the internet and the distractions of the outside world. You'll find you'll not only survive without the things you thought were absolutely necessary but also that you might even thrive.

Be relaxed

'Most of what we say and do is not essential. If you can eliminate it, you'll have more time, and more tranquillity. Ask yourself at every moment, "Is this necessary?"'
                                                                —Marcus Aurelius

'When force of circumstance upsets your equanimity, lose no time in recovering your self-control, and do not remain out of tune longer than you can help. Habitual recurrence to the harmony will increase your mastery of it.'
                                                                —Marcus Aurelius

It was November 2020 and I couldn't stop screaming. I'd just come off a Zoom pitch meeting with Netflix—where they had bought the concept of turning my book *Wellmania* into an eight-part comedy series, starring global sensation Celeste Barber. Netflix!! OMG! Netflix!! How was this *EVEN HAPPENING TO ME???!!!!!*

My excitement levels were off the charts. It was, for me, as they say, unprecedented. Not even in my wildest dreams did I ever think one of my books would be made into a Netflix series—particularly not one where I spend a lot of time lurking around monasteries trying to find some sort of elusive spiritual elixir. After the Zoom pitch ended with a 'yes', I danced around the lounge room, I popped champagne, I called my closest friends. I was euphoric. It felt almost chemical, but the feeling was *in me*, produced by me and all natural. I was high, high, high . . .

Finally, when I stopped screaming and before I raced down to Icebergs for celebratory cocktails, I stepped out into the backyard and lay on the grass in the sun underneath an enormous gum. I could feel the excitement like an electrical current. This new, manic energy coursed through me. I could barely contain it.

This huge feeling had a long tail. It was weeks before I came down and could wipe the smile off my face, such was my excess of happiness. But gradually the feeling settled and I returned to base-line. Well, at least for a little while. What followed was the opposite of that intense high, as I experienced an unusually sustained period of intense lows. Over the following six months, I experienced some spectacular failures and let-downs, and I felt them just as intensely as I felt the euphoria. It was a form of homeostasis, that ol' biological drive to balance things out, I suppose, but both ends of the spectrum were way too intense to comfortably contain. The highs were too high and the lows too low.

As well as the Netflix deal, I was working on a difficult novel that would later be abandoned, writing a weekly column for *The Guardian* and living through a global pandemic of a disease for which there had not yet been found a vaccine. It was hardly being a frontline worker or shovelling snow in a gulag, but these things came with their own pressures. Just as my body crackled with the highs, it felt every inch of the lows. In the lows I started having mysterious jaw pain. My teeth hurt. I was waking every morning at 4 a.m. and was unable to return to sleep. My right arm started aching, making computer work painful. I tried dozens of different treatments but it wouldn't heal. Unable to type, I tried dictating my columns, journalism and Stoicism notes through voice recognition software but it was a mess. Epictetus was recorded as 'Epic Tennis'.

When the wheels started falling off in various parts of my life, I plunged into a level of despair I hadn't experienced since the crazy days of my late teens and early twenties. Everything felt absurd and operatic. I was having my most successful year ever, while also having my most chaotic and horrendous year ever. My body was going on strike. I was grinding my teeth to dust in my sleep. It was a dark time.

This type of personal chaos was also being writ large across society. Lockdowns were starting and stopping all over the country—and everyone seemed to be going through a deranged version of the same manic highs and low lows. A late-night snap press conference by a state premier would announce a lockdown starting at midnight that night, and thousands of people would take to their cars or flood the airports trying to get home or get away. Others, watching at home and seeing their near future dissolve into yet another round of home schooling or furloughing their business, would be immobilised and fall into a vortex of distress, despair, worry and panic. Then—months, days, weeks later—the lockdown would lift and there would be pre-dawn crowds at Kmart and a bacchanalian atmosphere in the bars.

As time went on, the energy hectic, the weeks and seasons and old rhythms out of whack, it seemed like it was becoming harder and harder to regulate ourselves. What did *in between* feel like again? What did *normal* feel like? How could we get back into harmony? Could inner peace be obtained with such chaos happening outside? The mood—both collectively and for me as an individual—seemed to shift depending on what was happening externally (a massive Netflix deal, a global pandemic) and, attached as it was to these external rails, felt more akin to travelling on a roller-coaster than gliding on level tracks. I guess if you fix your mood to something outside you, then your inner state will always be outside your control.

I looked back on the euphoria of November and the despair of February and wondered if it was possible to use the Stoicism I was learning to help me not only in the bad times, but to also manage the good times.

Could it help me even things out a bit so I didn't feel so controlled by external things, I could get off the roller-coaster and not feel so wrung out by big shifts in mood or events?

This process of evening out my mood ended up being one of the biggest lessons in my Stoic journey. It boiled down to having a conscious awareness of my baseline mood, and regulating it according to ancient Stoic techniques and principles.

Seek tranquillity

Forget euphoria; the Stoics prized tranquillity above all other states. They had names for it—*ataraxia*, meaning 'a lucid state of robust equanimity characterised by ongoing freedom from distress and worry' and *eudaimonia* meaning 'unperturbed' (or, literally, 'without mental trouble').

Ataraxia is a word that has fallen out of modern usage—but shouldn't have. We need it more than ever! In our modern age where we reach for constant dopamine hits via reliance on technology, online shopping and social media, we are sorely in need of a steady, slow-release drug like ataraxia, with its positive effects accumulating over days and weeks.

Ancient philosophers believed achieving ataraxia created an emotional homeostasis, where the effect wouldn't just be a more stable base-level mood, but one that would, they hoped, flow out to the people around you.

If you are more tranquil, you will be less likely to react or combust. Not only do you not ruin your own day, you could avoid ruining other people's days too. In a tranquil state you may make better decisions. You're certainly likely to get less riled up and angry.

But how achievable is ataraxia—particularly for a modern person who is surrounded by disaster, disease, distraction, desires, marketing, social media, end-of-the-world vibes and the relentless demands of capitalism? Particularly if you are someone swayed by passions and crave the intense highs of the chase, say, falling in love or closing a deal?

When I wrote about ataraxia for *The Guardian*, I asked renowned British philosopher and author Professor A.C. Grayling for some suggestions about how to achieve ataraxia. 'Passion suggests something active to us,' he said. 'But if you look at the etymology of the term (passion), it's passive—it's something that happens to you—like love or anger or lust—that was visited on you by the Gods.'

Unlike passion, you create ataraxia, for 'peace of mind, inner calm, strength', Grayling said.

So when you face all the inevitables in life, all the shadows that are going to fall across life—such as losing people we care about, suffering grief, failing, making mistakes, feeling guilty—ataraxia is dealing with these shadows and being prepared for them. Preparation is a daily thing. But ataraxia is also learning how to relax and to have fun and making the most of each day. That also causes you to flourish.

Although the use of the word 'ataraxia' has fallen out of favour, 'it's just another way of saying "I've got to get my shit together",' said Grayling.

> When people say 'I've got my shit together' they mean 'I've got my balance and harmony', which is so crucial—we need it . . . at the moment . . . If you have things like lockdowns—particularly if you are in extended lockdowns—you have to find new levels, a new balance. And that takes a certain degree of psychological energy to ask 'what would it take for me to get there?'

In a widely shared Medium post, Stoic adherent Steven Gambardella wrote:

> Ataraxia is not a positively-defined state such as 'happy' or 'excited'. It was believed by the Hellenistic philosophies to be a 'resting' state of serenity. It is nevertheless a desirable state of mind, one that (Greek philosopher) Pyrrho believed that human beings naturally possess but can easily lose. In the same way that when free of illness our bodies are in a state of homeostasis, ataraxia is simply the *absence* of perturbation.

Speaking to me from his home in London, Gambardella expanded on this. 'In the modern world we are deeply unhappy because our understanding of happiness is incorrect. We think it will arise from doing something—from a positively designed state—drinking, having sex, shopping . . . This version of happiness is quite bound up with consumerism.'

Instead, said Gambardella, ancient Greek philosophers, such as the Epicureans, the Stoics and Sceptics 'taught that happiness is not a positively defined state—it is a negatively defined word. It's "without being phased", or having any kind of strong feelings—and the Ancient Greeks were obsessed with it.'

The theory of ataraxia 'emerged at a time of crisis . . . in the chaos and bloodshed that followed Alexander's (the Great) death'.

It 'is an objective for anybody seeking a sense of balance and calm, especially in times of uncertainty'.

This sounded a lot like now. It sounded like we all needed it, badly.

Happiness or tranquillity?

Andrew and I differed slightly when it came to how to approach this area of Stoicism.

I had begun to become suspicious of the concept of happiness—seeing it as a swing state that, before too long, ushered in its opposite—despair. If I started feeling too happy or too good about something, I braced myself for its corresponding negative binary. I started to think it was better to be tranquil, even, chill, relaxed. As Gambardella said, ataraxia is simply the *absence* of perturbation.

It follows: if you don't get too high, you won't sink too low.

Andrew argued that happiness per se wasn't the problem—you just couldn't tie happiness to anything external. So if I could only be happy if I got a Netflix deal, then I was tying my happiness to something outside my control. This was doomed to end badly for me, because it meant I could be thrown off course by externals, and be in turmoil because the object of my happiness is a moving target. I had tacitly agreed for someone else to control or sign off on my happiness.

Andrew told me he *trained* his happiness on things within his control. These things that he could control, of course, could only be one of three things: his character, his reactions/actions and how he treats others. The training element comes in by consciously steering pleasure and a satisfaction away from things that are not within his control.

By that definition, he was happy if his character was good, he kept his reactions in check, his actions were virtuous and he treated others well. These things were all within his control—and if he executed these things properly, then a feeling of happiness would follow. To move outside this, to seek happiness in money or fame, in external validation or in the affection of others, is to be on dangerous ground. All these things are outside his control, making his happiness contingent on someone else's actions.

Following Andrew's logic, you could guarantee your happiness by training it to be caused only by the things you could fully control.

Even things within our partial control do not guarantee happiness. For example: it might make me happy to go kayaking with a friend on Sydney Harbour. I look forward to it and the day comes around, but then there is an unexpectedly strong morning wind, or heavy rain, or the kayak place is shut, or my friend flakes on me— or all of the above. Suddenly something that seems like a sure-fire path to happiness—or at least pleasure—can end in disappointment. I have given away my power to external forces. But if I trained my happiness on the three things fully within my control, then I would be happy if I reacted well to disappointment and treated my friend positively, regardless of him cancelling on me.

So what should we be aiming for when it comes to mood? For Andrew it was happiness—but only a happiness that sprang from things within his control. For me, I took a different path and settled on tranquillity as something I could try to control, following the ancient Greek concepts of ataraxia and eudaimonia.

But both approaches lead to roughly the same outcomes: that is, not being a hostage to fortune and shaken by external events.

How to achieve ataraxia

The Stoics achieved ataraxia by using reason to assess a situation rationally, to understand what they could control, and what they couldn't control. Remember the earlier chapter on the control test? What you cannot control is not worth worrying about.

A.C. Grayling said ataraxia can be achieved if you 'have courage to face what is outside yourself, such as earthquakes, pandemics and natural disasters, old age and death. And if you have self-mastery of your inner self.'

Techniques to achieve ataraxia also include 'zooming out'—and seeing yourself and your problems as just small specks in a massive universe.

Steven Gambardella explained it this way: 'You "run with the stars" as Marcus Aurelius puts it—either by distancing yourself from your emotions or breaking things down in a way that allows you to dissect your emotions to understand what . . . issue is really at stake, and to understand that your passions are running away.'

The full Aurelius quote is beautiful: 'Dwell on the beauty of life. Watch the stars, and see yourself running with them.'

By controlling our fears and desires (in other words, our passions), we come closer to achieving tranquillity.

In practical terms, 'one of the main things we can do to try to achieve ataraxia is avoid social media,' Gambardella said.

'Instagram can make people feel sad and lonely. It is the perfect anti-ataraxia phenomenon. Because you could never be followed by enough people, you could never have enough Likes—it's based on this idea of super abundance . . . and it's filled with notifications that you should follow this complete stranger.'

But before we achieve ataraxia, first we need to discard the old positive notions of happiness as surplus or abundance.

'People have very shallow ideas about what happiness is,' Grayling said.

For example—being in love. One of the great cons in life is that being in love is what happiness is about. Then five or ten years later you wake up and go 'who the hell is this person?' If you are achieving a heightened emotional state that you get at a party or in infatuation—that is not happiness.

Happiness is a state and the state in question is where you, the individual, have a firm basis and place to do the work you need to do; the grief you need to go through; the people you need to encounter and the help you need to give people around you.

Yes.

How do I maintain tranquillity?

Like a lot in Stoic philosophy, there was no magic bullet for becoming more tranquil, except becoming more aware of my inner state and prioritising maintaining tranquillity over hedonism, fast thrills and high excitement.

To do this requires work. I continue to meditate twice a day, for 20 minutes at a time, and remind myself many times a day that I need to relax. I become conscious of sensations in my body that indicate

I'm feeling stressed, such as a tight feeling in my chest. I sleep when I need to sleep—so that I don't get my mind so worked up. The teeth grinding has slowed and I've also stopped feeling so manically happy that I can't sit still.

When I had some good news recently, one of my best friends was puzzled at my reaction. 'Why aren't you more excited?' she asked, in a vaguely accusatory tone.

But the truth was, with all this practising tranquillity, it was actually harder to get too excited about things. My reactions after a year of hardcore aiming for ataraxia tended to be more muted than before.

To be tranquil also requires being careful not to be too open to the opinions of others. Too much flattery can lead to an inflated sense of my own importance (flattery and a good reputation is out of my control, and to lose it could disrupt tranquillity), while too much criticism can lead me to feel upset. All this knocks my tranquillity out of balance. There is an irony in the fact that maintaining a quiet, tranquil state involves a bit of work—like a duck paddling furiously underwater in order to stay still and unruffled on the surface. But over time I have noticed that the longer I work towards tranquillity, the easier it becomes—and—this is the clincher—the easier *life becomes*.

In March 2022, the Netflix show that had caused me such a prolonged high started filming. I went to the first day of shooting on a quiet residential street in Concord. It was surreal seeing the catering trucks parked on a nearby oval, along with the make-up artists, and the camera operators, and the director, and the actors and the extras . . .

All these people here because of work I had done, in a quiet room in Castlemaine (the room where I am writing these words) in 2016.

Just before the director said, 'Action!' we had a Welcome to Country address from an Indigenous Elder and a smoking ceremony. As the smoke rose and spread, and, one by one, cast and crew walked through it, I felt a profound sense of gratitude, joy and pride for what was happening. It felt deeper and more grounded than the emotions that had coursed through me in November 2020 (going high, high, high and not landing—not for a long time), after our initial successful pitch with Netflix. The feeling didn't portend a later accompaniment by its opposite number, or be harmonised by a debilitating low. This was tranquillity in action. Being tranquil didn't mean I couldn't enjoy success and external things when they happened, it just meant I would also be okay if they didn't happen. It meant if there was no Welcome to Country, no cast and crew on that suburban Sydney street on that first day of filming because the project had fallen through, then I would be okay with that. My happiness doesn't depend on something outside me happening. Sometimes I'm stunned by the shift, as subtle as it sounds.

Benefits of tranquillity

There are other welcome by-products to being tranquil. For a start you care less what other people think about you because you realise what others say about you is out of your control.

As Marcus Aurelius explained tranquillity to himself in his diary: 'The tranquillity that comes when you stop caring what they say. Or think, or do. Only what you do.'

When you get rid of your fear of failure and what other people think, everything becomes more relaxed and fun. You just enjoy the ride.

A tranquil baseline state can also influence not just your reactions, but how you treat others. You are more likely to show good character and be less reactive if you are relaxed, even-tempered and easygoing about life.

Rich or poor, sick or well, famous or unknown, living in discomfort or living in a luxury home with all the mod cons, you should be able to achieve ataraxia regardless of your external circumstances. The tools are within.

In this important part of my Stoic journey, I realised that our lives and circumstances are always changing, things are always in flux—but throughout my life, if I make it a priority, my tranquillity can be protected from the slings and arrows—outrageous or otherwise—of life.

Be good

'The goal of life is living in agreement with Nature.'

—Zeno of Citium

'Waste no more time arguing about what a good man should be. Be one.'

—Marcus Aurelius

I t was late summer, 2022, and I was having a driving lesson in Kyneton, learning how to reverse park at the train station.

My instructor directed me to reverse in beside the only other car in the area—a grey van. As I squeezed in beside the van, I noticed a hand adjusting the curtains in the back window.

'Someone must be living in there,' I said to the instructor.

I squeezed out, paid for the lesson, then walked to the station to get a train home to the next town.

I noticed a person—it was the woman from the van—walking near me. She would have been in her seventies, white hair, a worn-out jumper and skirt, sandals.

'That was my first reverse park!' I told her. 'I'm going for my licence in eight weeks and, if I don't get it then, I will be the oldest learner driver in the world.'

The woman smiled, then did something truly odd. She came close to me, held out her hand and said, 'Take this.'

She was trying to hand me a 50-dollar note. Oh no. Please don't. I have found money on the ground before but no stranger has ever walked up out of the blue and tried to give me money. Particularly not someone who looked like they might need it themselves.

'I'm good, thanks. But thank you very much. That's very kind, but I don't need the money.'

'Please just take it,' she said. 'Take it.'

I sat waiting for the bus and started talking to the woman. Her name was Monica; she was from an opal-mining town in outback New South Wales and had travelled to central Victoria to see family.

She had tried to give money to other people—strangers—'but people don't want to take it'. She mimed someone putting up their hands and backing away from her like she was crazy. But she wasn't crazy. She just wanted to give people cash. She said that giving made her happy, and that the secret to a good life was not to want more than you have. 'If you are satisfied with what you've got, you'll have a good life,' she said. 'Too many people want what they don't have, so they spend their whole life working so they can get the next thing. But that doesn't make them happy—so they never get satisfied and they are always after more money to get the next thing that might make them happy.'

'And it never stops,' I said. 'The treadmill. The person is actually never satisfied. I guess that's capitalism . . .'

Monica nodded. 'I've always been happy with what I've got—so I've never wanted more.'

More was surplus—and so Monica gave away what she didn't need.

And she didn't need the $50 because she had been sleeping in her van at the station for three nights and so had saved money from van park fees.

'You can use the money for your next driving lesson,' she said.

My bus came and Monica and I wished each other luck. She walked back towards her van, taking it slow.

On the replacement bus service, I became completely undone.

What happened at the station seemed to go beyond a random act of kindness, but something more akin to grace. The money transcended the material and had become totemic, carrying something in it: character, kindness, a way of being in the world that I see so infrequently that the encounter felt almost holy. It was, I suppose, the pure goodness of Monica that struck me. She didn't want anything from me—she just wanted to give. It also made me wonder if *I* am good. Compared to Monica, the answer was 'no'.

Our culture is so built on hustle that everything feels transactional these days. That's why the encounter with Monica seemed so weird. Sure, people are nice to each other but, I wondered, is it because they want something in return?

You start at a new workplace and people are friendly but is it because they are subconsciously wanting to form alliances? Neighbours are kind; they invite you on their WhatsApp group but is it out of self-interest and the benefit in banding together to, say, fight the council application to build a telephone tower? People chat to you at a party but is it because they have no one else to talk to while they are waiting for their friends to turn up?

It feels easier to be cynical about people's motivations rather than just say 'people are good'.

Or maybe it's just me being transactional—and I am actually . . . *bad*. Ugh . . . I even feel uncomfortable just *thinking* about it.

I'm probably mostly self-interested, with random flashes of altruism, if I am to be honest. Recently, at a bar in Kings Cross, I was undercharged for some Campari and sodas. We could have got away with paying the lesser amount, but I drew attention to this to the waiter and paid extra. My friend said that was a 'good person act'; she wouldn't have said anything. But I was honest, 'because I don't want to get bad karma'. So even *that* is being transactional—in this case I want something in return for my goodness from the universe, in the form of good karma!

On giving

The Stoics tried to short-circuit the transactional nature of our relationships to others, by thinking hard about giving and reframing how we do giving and receiving of gifts. Seneca wrote his longest moral treatise, *On Benefits* (*De Beneficiis*) about how the impulse to give lies at the very heart of what it is to be human—otherwise we are no better than wild animals. Seneca saw gift giving as a way to emulate the gods, who gave us so many gifts in nature. He also sets out the best way to receive gifts, and that is with gratitude. This way of giving and receiving enhances our character and builds our virtue. In addition, according to Stoic principles, the giver of the gift should expect nothing in return (ideally a gift is given anonymously).

To give something with the expectation of a pay-off down the line, or quid pro quo is to forget the very foundations of Stoicism as laid out in the control test. We cannot control other people, or their actions, or responses. Therefore we cannot expect a response in return or a particular intensity or the presence of gratitude on behalf of the receiver, because their reaction is out of our control.

For example, if you've done a friend a favour by letting them stay in your house while you are away, you cannot expect that favour to be returned. You should not even expect your friend to thank you or leave a gift. You should give freely without expectation of any reward or gift in return. The same principle applies if you help someone find a job, or assist them when they are sick. This principle smashes up the transactional nature of our relationships with just about everyone. It makes giving less stressful, too. If you give without expectations of receiving anything in return, then you won't be disappointed when nothing comes your way (and maybe happily surprised when it does). And how should we give? 'We should give as we would receive, cheerfully, quickly, and without hesitation; for there is no grace in a benefit that sticks to the fingers,' wrote Seneca. Touché.

What is goodness?

But back to Monica—and her kind act of giving me 50 dollars. Would you do that? Questions of our own goodness are rarely interrogated, maybe because we have such blind spots around our own characters. Can we really look at ourselves objectively and say whether we are good or bad? We are a lot more at ease making an assessment as to whether *others* are good or bad people.

What sticks in my mind, partially pushed back into the recesses of memory, are all the times I've been awful. Yet some people I know tell me unbidden that I am a 'good person' or a 'good egg'. I always feel slightly surprised at this. What? Me? Really? Are you sure? *What even is 'good' anyway?* Is it giving away money when you have nothing? Is it looking out for each other in a more general way? And are we, as a species, inclined towards goodness?

The question has dogged everyone from Aristotle to Shakespeare to Hannah Arendt to Viktor Frankl. Just *what is* the bent of our human nature?

The ancient Stoics thought about these questions a lot. They believed that we are both oriented towards goodness (nature), and that we should strive for goodness (the virtues).

The Stoics also believed that we are both rational and social creatures, and that life flows better if we are 'living in agreement with nature'. This includes human nature as well as the natural world. We are born into families, societies, tribes, nations and a global community, and it is natural for us to be concerned for and care for others in our various communities. Ultimately that care of others should extend way beyond our immediate kin and encompass a care for all of humankind. The Stoics were very much anti-tribalist.

Greek Stoic Hierocles (c. AD 150) described Stoic cosmopolitanism through the use of concentric circles referred to as oikeiôsis. (Oikeiôsis in Stoic ethics signifies the perception of something as one's own, as belonging to oneself.) Hierocles described individuals as consisting of a series of concentric circles: the first circle is the human mind, next comes the immediate family, followed by the extended family, and then the local community. Next comes the community of neighbouring towns, followed by your country, and finally the entire human race. Our task, according to Hierocles, was to draw the circles in towards the centre, transferring people to the inner circles, making all human beings part of our concern. Those of you who have done a Buddhist 'loving kindness' meditation will recognise this concept. It can also be found in the ancient and mediaeval texts of Hinduism and Jainism.

As well as the principles of cosmopolitanism, the Greek and Roman Stoics wrote frequently and warmly about the joys of friendship and community. While Stoicism, on one level, is about fortifying yourself against suffering, many of the more solipsistic, inward-looking Stoic exercises and contemplations were to aid in a more harmonious outward expression of our nature, and were designed to make living with others more rewarding and less fractious. The Stoics believed we were better citizens, friends, partners, colleagues and fellow travellers if we were feeling good and tranquil within ourselves.

Are you a good person?

Over the course of three or so years of writing this book, I would randomly ask friends and acquaintances if they ever questioned whether they were a good person. Their answers often surprised me. People, whether or not they were cutthroat, or self-obsessed, or outwardly altruistic or selfish, charitable or mean—in short, all different types of people, with a range of personalities that lay across the moral spectrum—all answered that they spent some time reflecting on whether or not they were good people, and whether or not their actions were good or bad. What's more, being a good person was important to all of them.

Whenever I posed the question, people I asked told me they routinely calculated whether they were good people by the following metrics:

- whether the work they did made a positive, negative or neutral impact
- whether they were ethical in their dealings with others
- whether they acted ethically in relation to the environment, nature and other creatures such as animals
- whether they gave to charity
- whether they were a good and generous friend, parent, family member and child
- if they would leave the world a better place than when they arrived.

This widespread contemplation of goodness surprised me. What was their incentive to be good? Was it just a matter of squaring their own character with themselves? Being able to sleep at night? After all, none of the people I asked was particularly religious, so there was no incentive in the form of an afterlife to encourage their character to be good.

And I had a much broader discussion with a religious friend one lunchtime at a coffee shop in Chatswood. He was a devout Christian and just couldn't see the *point* of Stoicism. He asked, not unreasonably, because religion was my earliest moral lens, too: 'Are people *really* good for goodness's sake if there is no reward or punishment for their actions, no greater meaning than the fulfilment of our nature, giving the act of goodness a sort of animal impetus?'

There is original sin in all of us, he believed, and humans need more of a carrot or stick to be good people; that carrot or stick was missing in Stoicism.

119

Your character is one of the few things you can control, according to Stoic philosophy. But first—what does it mean to have a good character?

Character can be loosely defined as having moral and ethical qualities that guide your actions towards the greater good. It encompasses the way you treat others, your values and how you meet tests, adversity, challenges, largesse, excess (including money, food and booze) and how you behave out there in the world.

The material of character sustains us in difficult times—and 'furnishes (us) with a sustainable sense of self,' wrote sociologist Richard Sennett.

The importance of character has faded in recent decades. When I was a country lawyer, I would get my criminal clients to obtain a 'character reference' to hand to the judge or magistrate before sentencing, in the hope that someone of good character would be seen as being less likely to reoffend and would therefore attract a lower penalty. These small-town drug dealers, spousal abusers, drunk drivers and petty thieves would have to rustle up a letter from their parish priest or school principal to say they were of excellent character, and in fact their offence was actually *out of character*. They handed over the letter, then hoped for mercy from the bench.

That was the only time the question of character was explicitly considered in my day-to-day life. Instead, as I left the law and moved into journalism, more flashy attributes were prized and discussed: charisma, success, good looks, a cool vibe, being funny or smart.

Take politics. Once a stellar character was a prerequisite for a political career; now charisma rules and character is irrelevant. The British prime minister breached health orders by holding parties in Downing Street while the rest of the country 'stayed at home to save lives'. Trump's advice in 2005 about engaging with attractive women was to 'Grab them by the pussy. You can do anything!' A few weeks after that statement was made public, Trump was elected US president.

Having a bad character is incentivised every time a terrible person comes to power (particularly if they were democratically elected).

Maybe we don't elect 'good' people to public office anymore because we are suspicious of the very notion of 'good'. What does the word even mean now? In this relativist age, can one person's idea of good differ from another person's? And without the overarching bind or narrative of a common religion, is it now the case that each person carries around an essentially private and specific idea of what good is? Some people refer to the teachings of Jesus for their idea on what is good and others follow advice from a self-help guru like Tony Robbins and others from Oprah Winfrey or the Queen—or actors, or sports stars or the characters in the Harry Potter books or from the Marvel universe. Laws and rules provide an agreed-upon standard, an electric fence around the boundaries, that brings us back if we go too far but the rest is a matter between ourselves and our own conscience. So can we even talk about what is *good* these days?

How do we *know* if we are good?

When I asked my sample how they knew if they were being good or not, my sample did not refer to any religious text, dogma, teachings or philosophies. Instead they all talked about how they *felt*. That is, doing *good* made them *feel good*, and doing something bad made them feel—subtly or otherwise—*bad*. So, in other words, a subtle inner feeling will tell us if our behaviour is good or bad.

You can override this bad feeling by justifying your bad actions—for example, if you are taking revenge on someone or punishing *them* for being bad—but generally, most people's moral compass points in the same direction.

The Stoics called this compass, or this feeling, 'nature'—and believed it guides us to recognise and do good.

The Stoics frequently talked about 'living in agreement with nature'. This, in part, means that it is within our nature to be social, cooperative beings who want the best for others, and for people around us to thrive. Zeno of Citium, the founder of Stoicism, said, 'All things are parts of one single system, which is called nature; the individual life is good when it is in harmony with nature.'

It is not in our nature to want to see others suffer or be deprived, because if some of us suffer, then as social beings who live in a society, all of us suffer. 'What's good for the hive is good for the bees,' Marcus Aurelius wrote in *Meditations*.

The Stoics—being realists—recognised that it is also in human nature to act badly. But they believed this bad behaviour could be corrected or unlearned. 'Humans have come into being for the sake of each other, so either teach them, or learn to bear them,' said Marcus Aurelius.

HOW DO YOU HANDLE PEOPLE WITH BAD CHARACTERS?

Learning to bear people who had bad characters was something Marcus Aurelius was practised at. He would remind himself:

When you wake up in the morning, tell yourself: the people I deal with today will be meddling, ungrateful, arrogant, dishonest, jealous and surly. They are like this because they can't tell good from evil. But I have seen the beauty of good, and the ugliness of evil, and have recognised that the wrongdoer has a nature related to my own—not of the same blood and birth, but the same mind, and possessing a share of the divine. And so none of them can hurt me. No one can implicate me in ugliness. Nor can I feel angry at my relative, or hate him. We were born to work together like feet, hands and eyes, like the two rows of teeth, upper and lower. To obstruct each other is unnatural. To feel anger at someone, to turn your back on him: these are unnatural.

The virtues

We know that, according to the Stoics, character was one of the only things you could control in life (a life that was often harsh and unpredictable). Therefore you had a duty to create and maintain the best character you possibly could. A good character was one that cultivated what were known by Stoics as the four virtues: courage, self-control, wisdom and justice.

What's more, the pursuit of good character in ancient times excluded no one: man, woman, slave, freeperson, black, white. The Stoics believed that regardless of a person's circumstances or position in life, anyone could develop a good character. It was part of human nature, and with practice and commitment, these four virtues could flourish in each person.

For the ancients, having a good character not only made your own life easier (you could absorb the blows of fortune a bit easier with wisdom and courage), but it made life better for those around you. With self-control (or temperance) you were less likely to fly into a rage and upset others. With justice, you were committed to fair and equitable outcomes, not only for yourself but those around you. With wisdom you were able to counsel your friends and community as to correct courses of actions and with courage you were able to assist others and yourself in overcoming adversity.

The Stoics believed each of these four virtues was achievable— and that they are innate to everyone regardless of personality, because they are a part of our nature and capacity as humans.

You can be good, but you can't make someone else be good

Being a good person, or at least becoming a better person, became part of my Stoicism journey because it was one of the only three things in my complete control. Forget about trying to change other people to become good. You can be a role model or instruct and persuade people to be good, but it is ultimately not within your control as to whether someone is good or bad, or behaving well or poorly. As Marcus Aurelius advised: teach them, or learn to bear them.

This lesson was a tough one for me to swallow, particularly if I felt like getting angry at someone who had wronged me. Wasn't anger a way of signalling displeasure and boundaries? But Stoic teachings, particularly on anger, pointed out that someone else's bad character is up to them to rectify, not me. By stooping to the level of a badly behaving person by myself behaving badly to someone who has wronged me, I am just hurting myself and my own character.

Epictetus gave an example about a thief who stole a beautiful iron lamp from him. Epictetus replaced it with a cheaper earthenware one and said, 'The reason why I lost my lamp was that the thief was superior to me in vigilance. He paid however this price for the lamp, that in exchange for it he consented to become a thief: in exchange for it, to become faithless.'

What Epictetus lost was a lamp. What the thief lost was a lot more serious—his character.

How do I develop my character?

This is a hard one. It's a work in progress. But I trust that subtle, inner feeling that I was talking about earlier on. It's like a little invisible, but powerful pilot light that will ignite and alert me to when I am acting badly or when I am acting according to my best nature.

When I act in a way that is good, I feel good, and when I act in a way that is bad, I feel bad. It's really that simple. And when someone is good to me—as Monica from the train station was, giving me a random 50-dollar note—I feel better about the world, but also humbled. There are a call and response encoded into these things. Someone does a good turn to you. So what are you going to do for others? Goodness can be infectious—and that's how you develop your character and help influence the characters of the people around you.

MONITORING YOUR CHARACTER

You can keep an account of your character through diary keeping (like Marcus Aurelius and Seneca did), meditation and contemplation. With these practices you can work out where things are going well and where they are deficient. This is why reputation—or others' assessment of your character—is really not that relevant.

Maybe you can take on Seneca's advice with giving and receiving and start practising gratitude as well as giving without expecting anything in return. Note where you are behaving transactionally, treating another person as a mere vehicle to get where you want to go, and nip it in the bud.

And drop the scarcity mindset, where you think you are pitted against other human beings. This is most likely to lead to being closed, distrustful and hoarding things and resources for yourself. This is true on a personal level, as it is on a societal level.

How to . . .

Be untroubled

'People are not disturbed by things, but by the views they take of them.'
—**Epictetus**

'You have power over your mind—not outside events. Realise this, and you will find strength.'
—**Marcus Aurelius**

'You look at the pimples of others when you yourselves are covered with a mass of sores.'
—**Seneca**

'Why are people so weird lately?' headlined an article in *The Atlantic*. People were getting angry on planes and in airports; the unhinged dialogue on social media was spilling into real-life arguments; in their vehicles people were mowing down pedestrians in larger numbers than ever before; rates of drinking and drugging had increased. As the world eased out of pandemic restrictions, society wasn't snapping back to whatever normal used to be—people were acting too unpredictably (the Oscar slap!), and, well, weird.

'What on earth is happening? How did Americans go from clapping for health-care workers to threatening to kill them?' asked *The Atlantic*.

The reasons are complex but experts pointed towards stress, social ties being severed due to lockdowns and the increase in substance abuse, which lowers inhibitions, including moral and societal inhibitions.

All these behaviours—lashing out, being angry, threatening others, being obnoxious on social media—the Stoics would have argued are within our control to manage. They are our reactions (or actions) and one of the only three things completely within our control.

You could argue, as I did during my walks with Andrew, that reactions often come on too fast to manage or halt. But the counter-argument, made by the Stoics (and Andrew) was that as long as we possessed a rational mind, we could control our reactions and actions.

But first let's look at a crucial element that interacts with our actions and reactions: judgements.

What if things were just . . . neutral?

Judgements make reality good or bad. It's really that simple, and that difficult. We are—to a certain extent—our thoughts. We prefer some things over other things, and we order and categorise the universe into columns of 'good' on one side and 'bad' on the other. These judgements do not always represent the objective truth. We make judgements quickly, often without adequate information, or we are too fast to judge something that doesn't benefit from judgement or even require us to judge it. So much of what we label good or bad is actually neutral, but our judgements are powerful and dictate to a large extent how we respond to things. Said Marcus Aurelius of the criteria of 'good' and 'bad': 'You take things you don't control and define them as "good" or "bad". And so of course when the "bad" things happen, or the "good" ones don't, you blame the gods and feel hatred for the people responsible—or those you decide to make responsible. Much of our bad behaviour stems from trying to apply those criteria.'

I may think it's bad that I didn't get a house that I applied to rent— but why is that bad? I just wasn't successful. There may be another house on the market that is more suited to me. The house may have been beset with problems: things may have broken down, the land-lord may have been shoddy, there could have been an infestation of cockroaches. But I rush to make a judgement that something is 'bad' (missing out on the property) without being armed with all the facts.

UNCHECKED, WE ARE SWAMPED BY EMOTION

Our judgements are hugely important because they determine how we act. Using *reason* is a way we can gain some sort of mastery over the tide of emotions that could swamp us if left unchecked. We have more than 60,000 thoughts a day—some great, but many of them junk—and we need to use reason to sort through them before we act. We often ruminate on things that are troubling us (an upcoming meeting with our boss, for example) but all the rumination in the world will not change the course of the actual meeting. Preparation will. Rumination won't. When we ruminate over things and become obsessive, our thoughts become like junk food: bad for us, lacking in nutrition and unable to provide the energy we need to get things done. You don't eat junk food all day, so don't think junk-food thoughts.

Rational thinking

The Stoics put a huge store on our ability to think rationally. It is a power that is innate in every human being, the power to reason our way out of a heightened and often false emotional state.

Famously, Epictetus said, 'It's not what happens to you, but how you react to it that matters.'

This aspect of Stoicism seemed straightforward enough for Andrew, but it caused me a lot of angst. If emotions were that easily controlled by rational thinking, why were there wars, divorces, brawls, violence, disputes, lawsuits and broken friendships? 'It's not that simple!' I kept saying.

To get another perspective, I read the writing of modern-day philosopher Martha Nussbaum and her excellent work on desire and emotions and how they fitted into the ethical framework of the ancient Stoics.

In *The Therapy of Desire* she wrote: 'emotions have a rich cognitive structure. It is clear that they are not mindless surges of affect, but discerning ways of viewing objects; and beliefs of various types are their necessary conditions'.

The complexity of emotions and the unique personality of each individual they arise in mean that the Stoic command to control your reactions can seem simplistic. There's a lot of unconscious behaviour that drives emotions and judgements; unpicking and neutralising our emotions and judgements, as the Stoics advised, is one hell of a job. This area of Stoicism reinforced my gut feeling about some aspects of Stoicism: that is, it sets a high bar, too high for many of us, but gives us an ideal to aspire to and work towards.

But first let's look at how we might start to achieve that via dismantling some of our judgements.

Our judgements never cease

Our judgements can cause us a tonne of misery because we are constantly categorising things without realising it. We swim in a sea of negativity, our cognitive biases swinging towards pessimism a lot of the time but, according to the control test, it doesn't have to be this way. That is because we can always control our reactions to things.

Let's start with a typical day. You wake up and, depending on what sort of night's sleep you've had and what sort of day you have ahead, your mind will already be racing to put a label on how you feel the minute you are awake. If you slept badly, with strange dreams and a kink in your back, maybe you've already started labelling your experiences as 'bad'.

Rolling over to your phone, you check the news, weather and social media. Bad. Bad. Bad. In the news—which is almost always about things going wrong in the world—you see that there is a war that is causing chaos and death. The weather forecast is for clouds and afternoon storms. Your mood drops even further. When will this rain ever stop? Then on social media, you see an opinion you tweeted was misinterpreted and you are being attacked. You immediately feel defensive and under siege. You switch tabs and see that you have been praised in a staff email about a project you were involved in. Suddenly you feel good. Then you check your bank account. You've been paid! Good!

Before you have even encountered anyone—before you have even got out of bed!—you have made half-a-dozen judgements that have changed the shape of your day. But in reality, did you have to judge any of them? Aren't many of the things that we encounter totally neutral? Aren't we able to just acknowledge their existence and let them pass without having to put a label on them?

If we don't form a judgement about something, we're less likely to ruminate on it (in the case of something 'bad') or cling to it and become attached (in the case of something 'good'—like praise from your boss or a client).

When we make no, or fewer judgements, we are more liable to just let life unfold and experience things in a non-reactive, open way. Tasks, relationships with others and just the experience of life become a lot easier when you're not loading every little thing up with a judgement. Things don't get stuck. We're not anxiously dwelling on something that went wrong on Monday when it's Thursday and the thing that upset us has long since passed.

It's that simple: when we stop labelling things, life suddenly gets a lot easier. It just happens. One thing follows the next, and we don't get stuck.

Just think how much easier your job would be if you didn't go around judging your co-workers as your competition, your boss as a monster or the work you've been given as a tedious burden.

Not judging things doesn't mean that you leave your brain or intuition at home, and refuse to take in information or cues; it just means that we try to not put a judgement on *every little thing*.

Life is for us

The Stoics—as well as Taoists, yogis and spiritual teachers such as Eckhart Tolle—believe that life is for us, not against us, and that, if we resist it, we will miss out on the ease and bounty of life. We instead get stuck in a negative pattern of resistance, negativity, strain, struggle and pain.

Said Marcus Aurelius:

> True understanding is to see the events of life in this way: 'You are here for my benefit, though rumour paints you otherwise.' And everything is turned to one's advantage when he greets a situation like this: You are the very thing I was looking for. Truly whatever arises in life is the right material to bring about your growth and the growth of those around you. This, in a word, is art—and this art called 'life' is a practice suitable to both men and gods. Everything contains some special purpose and a hidden blessing; what then could be strange or arduous when all of life is here to greet you like an old and faithful friend?'

The Stoics in their innate wisdom realised the importance of mastering our perception of the world. We can get lost in our judging mind. The Stoics sought out true and objective beliefs (using their powers of rationality), not unnecessary value judgements.

We are often harshest on ourselves

Perhaps the most pervasive and toxic form of judgement is that which we heap on ourselves. We wouldn't talk to our worst enemy the way we often talk to ourselves. An example: I was feeling tired in the middle of the day. It was close to Christmas and I'd had a big year. I could take a break, and sleep for an hour to refresh. I did—but I did it with a lot of self-judgement. As I got into bed and set my alarm for an hour,

I cursed myself for being weak for needing a nap. I labelled myself lazy for not being able to work through fatigue on a hot afternoon; I cursed my body and mind for letting me down and needing rest. It was only when I woke up feeling more refreshed that I clocked all the negative judgement I had heaped on myself for a totally harmless one-hour nap. I realised I needed to be aware of how I was talking to myself because my inner judgement of myself had elevated to quite harsh, uncompassionate levels without my realising it.

So how do we learn to let go of judgements?

Become aware of your reactions

Our judgements and our reactions are closely linked. We make a judgement then we react (or it can happen the other way around—we have a reaction and then put a judgement on it). Sometimes our reactions are purely physiological: we burn our hand on the flame, so we remove it quickly from the stove. Other reactions are psychological and come from our judgements.

How we react depends on whether we think something is good or bad.

Think about your reactions to things. Most reactions are totally unconscious but would follow a cycle of action, reaction, contraction, without our even being consciously aware of it. You have the action: let's say, for example, you argue with your spouse or roommate about housework. *They're not helping out at all! You do most of the work!* Then the reaction: the argument makes you angry. Then the contraction: you withdraw and stew on what you perceive.

That is our usual unconscious pattern that gets repeated in conflict. The Stoics believed that reactions are in our control, so we therefore have the ability to break this unconscious reactive conflict cycle.

While you cannot change how people treat you, you can change how you react.

Controlling your reactions

You can control your reactions to situations but it is not always easy.

Say you are in a minor car accident, and the other driver has a meltdown and starts abusing you. What is within your control is how you react. In this situation, the best reaction is to keep calm and not to lose your cool. Remember: action, reaction, contraction. You can't contract if you don't react.

You might argue that of course you are going to react if someone insults you. After all you are not a robot.

It *is* normal to have feelings and emotions arise. Probably bad vibes would arise if, in the case of the minor car accident, the other driver was screaming at you. But you can use your judgement and decide that since you can't control what he thinks of you or what he says, there is no point in worrying about it or being reactive.

Anyway, already, by insulting you, he has damaged his character—which is the gravest thing that can happen according to the Stoics.

Said Marcus Aurelius, 'It can only ruin your life only if it ruins your character. Otherwise it cannot harm you—inside or out.'

How do you stop yourself from reacting to an insult?

You stop yourself from reacting to an insult or aggressive behaviour by keeping check of your emotional reaction. There are two major forms of emotion: those arising from what the Stoics called 'impressions', and those arising from our judgements. Impressions are often not within our control. They are almost physiological in origin, like a blush or the hot-stove example I gave earlier. This is opposed to a judgement, which you can control.

An impression is an initial reaction, almost an animal instinct, for fear, or mistrust or desire or envy or pleasure. A Stoic would register the impression, but then use her reason to override it, should it disrupt her tranquillity or not serve her in some way. So if you have a reaction, say fear at a loud, unexpected noise, but then it turns out to be a car tyre blowing out nearby, you adjust your reaction, so you don't feel afraid, the impact of the impression is slight, and as a result, there is no contraction. You have not been knocked out of that tranquil zone that should be your baseline resting state.

You can't control impressions but you shouldn't respond impulsively to them either, say the Stoics. Epictetus said, 'Remember, it is not enough to be hit or insulted to be harmed, you must believe that you are being harmed.' He also said, 'if someone succeeds in provoking you, realise that your mind is complicit in the provocation'.

That is why it is essential that you not respond impulsively to impressions. Take a moment before reacting, and you will find it easier to maintain control.

The early Greek Stoic Chrysippus likened emotions to running too fast. Once you get going and are fully in the rhythm of an emotion, it's hard to stop. The idea is to slow down your emotions—or at least become conscious of them as they are arising—and, in slowing them, recast or reassess your judgement. The Stoics call this technique 'reframing'.

For example, you could think—or make a judgement—that a colleague who grunted when you said hello to them in the morning doesn't like you or is unhappy with you. How often do we do that?

Probably more often than we think. That negative response to the grunt could be your initial judgement. Stoicism asks that you purposefully slow that emotion and judgement and reframe it. Do you really have enough information to know if the abrupt greeting was because of something you had done? Perhaps it had nothing to do with you? Perhaps your colleague was having a terrible day or had just had a fight with their spouse before they left for the office or perhaps they have an important work meeting coming up that involves some tricky conversations about their contract? You don't know what's going on for that person—yet so often we rush to make a judgement. We make it all about us.

Perhaps you're like me and constantly feuding with people in your head because of the way they had looked at you or talked to you. These thoughts, unfounded in any real information, often arise because I'm too quick to judge a situation.

The consequences can suck. Unless we reassess an initial judgement, we are stuck with these faulty beliefs and muddled first impressions running around in our heads. Perhaps you'll carry around that poor judgement with you all day—ruining your day—and making you paranoid and insecure. Maybe you are rude to other co-workers because you are preoccupied by this so-called slight. 'Roger hates me'—you'll tell yourself, when in actual fact Roger might have been up all night with a sick child and has a meeting with the union in the afternoon about his hours being cut. Roger didn't even *see you* when you said 'hi'.

A fast judgement can produce negative emotion. As well as carrying around a false story about your colleague all day and creating an enemy in your own head, you have also significantly disrupted your tranquillity. The reason a Stoic guards against making hasty judgements is so tranquillity is maintained. You are less likely to be disturbed internally if you refrain from going around and labelling everything that crosses your path.

Seneca knew this when he said, 'it is not the wrong that is done that matters but how it is taken'. Marcus Aurelius also wrote about how the products of a faulty judgement can cause us pain. He said, 'if you are distressed by anything external the pain is not due to the thing itself but to your estimate of it—and this you have the power to revoke at any moment'. So take your power back!

USING RATIONALITY AND THINKING AHEAD

At first glance, it's easy to imagine that to deny or suppress a feeling would cause some sort of psychological problem down the line. But this technique is less about suppressing feelings more than using your rationality to assess whether pursuing the feeling is going to lead to suffering.

What happens if you don't judge a situation?

Without judgement there follows acceptance of a situation as it is. Judgements can cause resistance, which leads to a lack of acceptance about the present moment.

Without judgements we avoid the 'should have' loop: my boss *should have* given me a pay rise or my husband *should have* helped with dinner. Instead we just accept the situation—the present moment—as it is. An acceptance of the present moment, without judgement, comparisons or fear can be transformative. We are suddenly not fighting with life, wishing it were different, and rejecting what we have. Marcus Aurelius wrote (in one of my favourite lines), 'Accept the things to which fate binds you, and love the people with whom fate brings you together, but do so with all your heart.'

What should we judge?

Let's look at the control test again for this one. We have no control over how other people act or their reactions, so our judgement over them is unlikely to be helpful or effectual. Being judgemental about someone else is not guaranteed to change them or their behaviour, because their behaviour is not up to us. Also—as all of us would know—we can feel it when someone is being judgemental towards us, and it can be very unpleasant.

Instead of trying to control others, a Stoic would try to persuade someone to adjust their behaviour, or act as a role model so that the other person can mirror or copy a different set of behaviours.

An example of this might be—you live with someone who drinks too much. They routinely get wasted a few nights a week and then ruin the evening plans you've made by being too drunk to do anything. As a consequence, you go to bed upset and agitated.

You can judge that person for drinking (it would be difficult not to!). But you do *not* have control over that person's drinking: it is up to them. You can persuade them that drinking too much is harmful (this is both a judgement and a fact) but the best you can do is model correct behaviour. If you are having a go at someone drinking, while you are also drinking a bottle or so of wine a night, then it's unlikely to encourage someone else to stop or slow down.

Instead a Stoic would caution against judging something which isn't up to us. The only thing to judge is *what is up to us*—and that is our own actions.

Without being too harsh or punishing ourselves, the only person you should judge is yourself. After all, you are the person whose character you know best, and you, more than anyone, should have a clear picture of what you've done, why you've acted a certain way and what the consequences of your actions have been.

Epictetus summed it up when he said, 'We are not privy to the stories behind people's actions, so we should be patient with others and suspend judgement of them, recognising the limits of our understanding.'

Hard as it may be, you have to not let the other person's drinking disturb you. You can certainly try to persuade them not to drink, but once you've done that, there's no point sulking, arguing or stewing about their behaviour. People can only directly control their own actions, not the actions of others.

What criteria should you use for judgement?

Trying to find the truth of the matter—and looking beyond your subjective judgements—is the key to living in reality.

Marcus Aurelius wrote, 'Everything we hear is an opinion, not a fact. Everything we see is a perspective, not the truth.'

How to be guided by reason and not by desires or judgements? How to live in reality, not a fantasy world? How to be awake, not asleep? How to see the world for how it really is—not how you want to see it?

How we see and process the world around us differs from person to person. I take in the world from my point of view, it flows in through my senses and therefore everything I experience is via my perception. All this is so automatic—this perception, where everything is judged in relation to myself, that I don't even really question my perspective. Our own individual blind spots are how much we really centre ourselves in our experiences of the world. We see ourselves as the star of the show; our perception informs how the show unfolds, and those around us are our co-stars or bit players in the dramas of our lives.

So little do we really think about perception that it can be quite jarring to be reminded that everyone else is walking around thinking *they* are the star of the show, and we are but a bit player in *their* lives. Everyone is living with their own view of reality. No wonder it can feel difficult to really connect with people; it's easy to feel separate or alienated, or to feel disappointed and let down when other people don't treat us in accordance with *our* perceptions and expectations.

The notion of perception is important to take into account for a number of reasons.

Your perception may be faulty

Your perception may be wrong—and as a result, you do not see the world as it is, but according to some incorrect position or projection that you hold. This can be the case in asymmetrical relationships—a not uncommon thing, where you are invested more in the other person than they are in you. You may think a person is a special friend or has a unique understanding of you, or your relationship is more intense and intimate than other friendships—but what a shock to discover that (more frequently than we might realise) the other person doesn't think of you much at all! Your realities are completely unaligned. While they are the main co-star in your show, you barely get a scene in theirs. A study by Abdullah Almaatouq and his colleagues in the Media Lab at the Massachusetts Institute of Technology in 2016 has shown that only half our friendships are mutual: 'When analysing self-reported relationship surveys from several experiments, we find that the vast majority of friendships are expected to be reciprocal, while in reality, only about half of them are indeed reciprocal. These findings suggest a profound inability of people to perceive friendship reciprocity, perhaps because the possibility of non-reciprocal friendship challenges one's self-image.' Blame for this blind spot was put squarely at the feet of faulty perception.

Your perception may not be shared

The understanding that those around us may interpret the world with vastly different perceptions—some of which may be faulty and others that are correct—can help us navigate communal life with more skill. It can assist us in better understanding disagreements in our society—in everything from the division of labour in a household and raising children to vaccine mandates and election results.

In an era of fake news and widespread misinformation that affect the very core of democracy and the notion of *truth itself*, examining our perceptions and beliefs—turning them over and holding them to the light—matters more than ever. So does understanding that other people hold different perceptions and realities—and that they act accordingly. That is, they act as if their view of reality is the correct one. We can understand, and perhaps be more compassionate to people, if we can see where they are coming from, even if their starting premise is false or one we disagree with. We can apply reason and clarity to their perceptions to get to the truth.

Perceptions can be changed

You can change your experience of the world by realising that your perceptions, and your place in the world can be changed and improved by adjusting your focus and your clarity. Ask: how much of reality do we imbue with emotions and judgements? 'A thing is not good or bad, it is thinking that made it so,' wrote Shakespeare in *Hamlet*, echoing a Stoic tenet. Perceptions can be changed by addition of new information or by stringent self-examination, stripping away the fantasies and wishful thinking you might have. This process involves examining emotions and judgements you may bring to a situation or person whom you may not be seeing clearly.

Just think about when you last had a crush on someone. You probably started thinking they were the handsomest, wittiest, smartest person you'd met. But when the crush wears off, our perceptions change—and the object of desire falls off their pedestal. We begin to notice that they just talk about themselves all the time, or they have a wonky nose. Whatever it is, the person is still the same, but your perceptions have changed. It's the same in many a romantic relationship that relies on mutual elevation, through the imagination, of each other's good qualities. When the trick of imagination—or perception—falters, so too can the relationship.

When you truly commit to examining your perception, using rationality and reason, the result is like getting a new pair of glasses that have a more powerful and accurate prescription. You can just see things better. Everything becomes clearer, including the way forward. When we see things clearly, we can also see a way out or a way through a difficult situation.

Like many things discussed so far, changing our perceptions to bring them more in line with reality—and less in line with our subjective experience—is a matter of bringing our conscious awareness to a situation and examining our thinking (including our biases and motivations).

Let life unfold

Being aware of reality means not crowding or loading up our perception with personal issues, wants, desires, stories, group identities and grievances—instead letting life just unfold and taking stock of it via our reason.

That is not what happens to most of us. Reality unfolds but gets stuck. We load it up with our judgements; we have a powerful subconscious influencing our thoughts and actions; we have memories and triggers; we have desires or want more from the present moment than it is providing; we have reactions, projections, and old sore spots that get triggered.

We create a story around things or people—and it is the story, not the thing itself, which creates our disturbances or our desires. Said Seneca: 'It's not activity that disturbs people, but false conceptions of things that drive them mad.'

This 'false conception' that Seneca spoke of is the story we carry around in our head. Or as Irish poet W.B. Yeats put it in 'The Circus Animals' Desertion', 'It was the dream itself enchanted me.' This story, this dream or this enchantment wouldn't pass any test of reason. It's a fantasy. Marcus Aurelius wrote, 'Regain your senses, call yourself back, and once again wake up. Now that you realise that only dreams were troubling you, view this "reality" as you view your dreams.'

Avoiding suffering by knowing reality

Many different philosophies and religions have incorporated the problems and perils of our individual, flawed perceptions in their teachings.

Great spiritual teachers knew the suffering that could result from perceptions that are misaligned with reality (or nature).

The Jesuit priest Anthony de Mello said one of the most important shifts a person can make is to recognise 'reality' instead of existing in a fantasy of subjective perception. He says, 'Wake up. When you're ready to exchange your illusions for reality, when you're ready to exchange your dreams for facts, that's the way you find it all. That's where life finally becomes meaningful. Life becomes beautiful.'

Isn't that something we all want? For life to be beautiful?

Seeing the world as it really is (what de Mello called 'reality'; what Aurelius called 'waking up') is a key part of Stoicism. As Marcus Aurelius put it in his journal, 'The first rule is to keep an untroubled spirit. The second is to look things in the face and know them for what they are.' (Or as Michael Cunningham wrote in *The Hours*, in an echo of Stoicism: 'To look life in the face. Always to look life in the face and to know it for what it is. At last to know it. To love it for what it is, and then, to put it away.')

Looking at the reality of a situation, being clear-sighted, having clarity, looking things in the face is the key to less suffering, not more. We fear the pain of looking something right in the face, particularly if it's a reality that might scare us or dislodge a fantasy that we had about our life. A common thing here might be the diagnosis of an illness with poor prognosis—maybe three months to live. Who wants to digest that news unvarnished and straight up?

Wouldn't it be better to have it softened? To be given hope? But a tough situation calls for courage, not a dilution of reality. We need to be told what the reality is, then meet it with courage and wisdom (and wisdom never flourished without truth) in order to overcome a tough situation.

Reality can't hurt us

We often don't want to see reality because we think it might hurt or upset us. But it won't. It's liberating to stop living in a fantasy world; in the end, *acknowledging reality* causes less suffering. When we look reality in the face there are no surprises or upsets because everything is in front of us. Taking off the rose-coloured glasses and seeing that the world contains suffering as well as joy, loss as well as gain, death as well as life—and that we will be subject to all these things—is the key to this clarity.

When we commit to facing up to reality, we find we are less surprised or upset by things, because we have been looking at them in the face, due to our clear perception. 'How ridiculous and how strange to be surprised at anything which happens in life,' says Marcus Aurelius of the clarity that illuminates.

The criteria to apply when judging yourself

That's how we should see reality; how about how we should see ourselves? Well, also clearly and realistically—but we should measure ourselves and our progress according to an internal set of principles. Stoics judged themselves according to Stoic principles. They asked: am I aligned with nature? Am I using or cultivating the four virtues of wisdom, temperance, justice and courage? Am I tranquil? Do I use reason? What state is my character in?

In order to make effective judgements on themselves (as opposed to unthinking automatically negative judgements), Stoics committed to exercises such as journalling, contemplation and self-examination.

Each night Seneca wrote in his journal, examining his day, how he acted and whether he could improve. And, famously, Marcus Aurelius wrote his personal thoughts and observations in a journal he titled 'To Himself' (*Meditations*). This journal was a self-examination of how his own character held up to the tests of the day according to Stoic principles.

People across the world and down through history have turned to the *Meditations* for solace, guidance and clarity.

Balancing emotions and reason

I agree with philosopher Martha Nussbaum: emotions are complex and not just 'mindless surges of affect'. I also agree with Andrew (and Chrysippus), in that slowing down reactions and judgements leads to a response that is more rational than instinctive. This can be very much to our benefit, the benefit of the other person and the benefit of society as a whole. We need fewer angry, reactive people in the world, not more. (I'll talk more about anger in the next chapter, 'How to be Calm', as the Stoics devoted a lot of time and energy to examining it.)

Slowing down an emotional response is not the same thing as ignoring strong feelings of intuition or being emotionless. The Stoics strove to experience emotions like joy and contentment but they took care to try to mostly stay on an even keel. They questioned the negative judgements that can lead to upsetting emotions. Wouldn't it be better to remove upsetting emotions? Wouldn't you prefer a life that was high on positivity and joy and low on negativity and suffering? This is possible if you try to master your judgements.

Keeping an eye on judgements means that you are less likely to be upset—and more likely to maintain that much desired tranquil state. As we've discussed, tranquillity was very important for Stoics. They lived in brutal times and there was so much that was not in an individual's control. But the ancient Greek and Roman Stoics, highly sophisticated thinkers, recognised that if they maintained a tranquil baseline, what happened that was outside their control would and could not rattle them so much, it wouldn't hurt and they could make the most of their one precious life here on earth.

The Stoics also sought to live in reality, not a fantasy land. They recognised that our minds and our imaginations created false hurts for us to dwell on: imagined slights or insults, grievances and grudges that had long since passed (like the example of misinterpreting a colleague's unfriendly greeting). As Seneca said, 'We suffer more in imagination than in reality.' How much we suffer is actually up to us.

Damn desire

The main problem with judgements that I kept butting up against was desire. We are programmed biologically, unconsciously and neurologically to desire certain things. Desire can be strong, even overwhelming at times, and all the rationality in the world can be puny when trying to dislodge some desires, especially romantic and sexual desires. Then there is the question: do we even want to override desire? Martha Nussbaum asked, not unreasonably, how you can have a passionate life if you are suspicious of passions: 'Can one live in reason's kingdom, understood in the way the Stoics understand it, and still be a creature of wonder, grief, and love?'

I wanted to be a creature of wonder, grief and love. Life is not worth living, otherwise.

At the end of life, we should be worn out with love—exiting having not lived carefully but with all our heart. How does living a passionate life square with Stoicism's insistence on rationality?

We can try to train our rational brain to be our first responder, but how realistic is that *all the time*? What about the first time you clap eyes on the love of your life, or the feeling you get when your child is born and you know you would commit murder for them if you must?

Ultimately I think the Stoic use of rationality can help lessen suffering coming from desire, but it can't eradicate it entirely. We're more complicated than that. Dreams, strange impulses, intuition, slips of the tongue, inexplicable behaviour—all indicate an area below consciousness that bubbles away and is resistant to the application of reason.

Rational thinking is not our only operating system in play. *Inexplicable behaviour* is part of the human condition. We are not AI (yet), able to program out all the troublesome parts of our responses and our desires, although the ancient Stoics tried in their brilliant way to design an early version of code, to help make us less susceptible to love's hurts, rejections and vulnerabilities, and sudden and downward changes in fortune.

So much work has been done on neuroscience, brain chemistry and psychology since the Stoics formulated their code thousands of years ago. Desire is a strong, often biological driver that can overcome rational thought with ease. How often have you or your friends ended up with a terrible, unsuitable partner, because the rational part of your brain was no match for your desires? Chrysippus said to slow your reactions, to give rationality breath and space to come in. But what about our human nature? It is in our nature to love like crazy and grieve like wild.

I do use the Stoic approach to rationality and I have definitely tempered my judgements a lot more since embarking on this Stoic journey. But around desire and love, I am an imperfect Stoic.

It's not just love and sexual attraction, but also grief. We'll get to grief in Part 3, but the animal part of our nature, and our wild, unruly hearts, can be tough to tame. Then there's the question: for all the pain of love and grief, would we have it any other way?

Part 2

LIFE AND
ITS ABSURDITIES

'There is no easy way from the Earth to the stars.'

—Seneca

'Look back over the past, with its changing empires that rose and fell, and you can foresee the future too.'

—Marcus Aurelius

'When you think you've been injured, apply this rule: If the community isn't injured by it, neither am I. And if it is, anger is not the answer. Show the offender where he went wrong.'

—Marcus Aurelius

Life was changing. The Stoics taught me it always did, and to move with the change. I left the house in Tamarama, with its bathtub in the backyard, towering ghost gum, burning bundles of sage in the hall and harmonium-playing housemates. The sublet was ending and it was time to return home to Victoria. Change was in the air, the vibe was that maybe the pandemic was winding down (it wasn't) and life would get back to normal (it wouldn't). I would miss the beach and the impromptu Stoic walks with Andrew—but he was moving away from the beach too.

For everything, there is a season.

This next part of the Stoic journey I would need to do on my own. In the words of Hecato, the Greek Stoic philosopher whose writing now exists only in fragments: 'What progress, you ask, have I made? I have begun to be a friend to myself.'

I was getting into the swing of things with Stoicism. I had now mastered the basics and was applying the theory to my own life. I had begun to be a friend to myself.

Soon I noticed shifts in how I saw the world and dealt with stress, but they were mostly subtle, imperceptible to the outsider. But there were shifts, nonetheless.

I was starting to run things through a Stoic lens, keeping a notebook with me so I could draw a flow chart of the control test when I was anxious about something or needed to make a decision. And I kept the preferred indifferents front of mind when I started to cling to things that I could lose at any time.

But I still struggled with regulating my emotions. Desire was still desire—and all the Stoicism in the world wouldn't change that. But I now knew where desire could lead: to attachment; to wanting something or somebody who was out of my control; to having my tranquillity disturbed. When desire reared its head, I tried to employ Stoic rationality (the water to desire's oil) and found some measure of detachment.

As the months passed, I also noticed my temperament start to even out. Was this mellowing related to age or was this Stoicism? Whatever it was, I was becoming more chilled. But for the most part, Stoicism was still not coming naturally to me. I had to really work at it, remember to use it, go back to the essentials and the theory. It was a bit clunky—and I often felt like a kid trying to learn to ride a bike.

At what point, I wondered wearily, does one transition from practising Stoicism from time to time, to *becoming Stoic*?

Apart from posting Stoic quotes on Instagram, and talking about the philosophy with Andrew, I hadn't really shared much Stoicism with others since the days of my WhatsApp group in 2019. But then, in mid-2021, my friend and colleague Jo got really sick. And I mean REALLY SICK. In the previous month, she hadn't been feeling well, 'some mystery stomach thing', she told me. It was lockdown in Sydney 2021, and we'd been for a walk around Redfern and Surry Hills, at the point where our 10-kilometre radiuses intersected. It was winter, cold and the late afternoon sky was monochrome white and grey. After hearing about how grim the hospital had been, we talked about our shrinking lives in lockdown: what we were reading, cooking, watching, thinking, streaming. Everything felt as muted as the sky. On the walk Jo looked a bit pale, and was walking slowly, but otherwise seemed okay.

Once she returned home from the walk, Jo started experiencing severe pain and had to be taken back to hospital. After a week of tests, she was found to have bowel cancer and required surgery followed by chemotherapy. Jo was an otherwise healthy 36-year-old, and this horrifying news was out of the blue. As a much-loved member of our newsroom and general all-round popular person in the Sydney media scene, everyone who knew Jo was thrown into disbelief and shock. Even though we could not come together in person, our community rallied: people cooked for Jo, dropped in presents, dropped over beers for her boyfriend, sent her books and maybe some even prayed for her. What could I do, apart from feeling helpless? Maybe . . . I could offer to teach her about Stoicism? (Although of course, as it turns out, through her lived experience, she had a lot to teach me.)

But yet, I hesitated. Did someone who was scheduled for major surgery followed by six months of chemotherapy really want to hear what some long-dead dudes from almost 2000 years ago said? And would it even be a consolation? A lot of Stoicism was harsh and unyielding. Someone suffering, in pain, isolated (Covid meant we couldn't visit) and lying in a hospital bed surrounded by others who were also in pain, might not necessarily feel cheered up by Stoicism. After all, it wouldn't be a distraction, but rather the opposite—it would challenge Jo to confront the reality of her situation.

Teaching Jo Stoicism also contradicted something Epictetus said: 'Don't explain your philosophy; embody it.' The ancient Stoics, unlike Christians, were not keen on proselytising their beliefs. Better to never mention Stoicism, and just go about your business *being a Stoic*, and then others would learn from you by emulating you, not by hearing a lecture from you.

And another thing, I wasn't a Stoic—not yet, anyway. *I was trying*, but it was hard. Maybe some Stoicism tutorials would help both of us?

Jo said she was interested in learning about Stoicism and so most days for the time she was in hospital and later home recuperating, I would record a voice note on WhatsApp and send it to her, so she could listen to it at her leisure. Each note contained a Stoic lesson, starting from the control test, moving to preferred indifferents, and on to dealing with setbacks and then the more modern life hacks— such as dealing with FOMO and finding her inner citadel or inner fortress, when in a crowded public hospital ward. Here are a few extracts from our WhatsApp conversation.

Tuesday, 3 August, 7.13 p.m.
Brigid: Heeey, Jo, it's Brigid. Just going to do some tiny little Stoic lessons that you can listen to when you feel like it—but the first thing I was going to tell you about is the control test . . .

Tuesday, 3 August, 10.35 p.m.
Jo: Loved this and also it should be a podcast.

Wednesday, 4 August, 8.47 a.m.
Brigid: Good morning, Jo. How's things? This note is just one building on the control test . . . let's look at character, what did they mean by that. The Stoics believed that you could work on it, change it, and they believed a good character comprised the four virtues . . .

Friday, 6 August, 7.00 a.m.
Brigid: Morning, Jo, hope you are well and the operation went well.
I hear it was a great success. Now . . . Stoicism. We have covered
the control test, character and virtues, and now today we'll look
at preferred indifferents.

Stoics say it's preferable to want to be healthy, wealthy and for
people to think well of you, but those three things are outside our
control—and while it may be good to have these things, they can
be taken from you at any time. It's important to really work out
what you can and can't control and if you can't control it, then you
should not worry about it. Health, wealth and reputation comes
into these categories of things that are outside your full control.

Sunday, 8 August 8.05 a.m.
Jo: All caught up now, loving these.

Monday, 9 August, 10.57 a.m.
Brigid: Hey, mate, how are you going? I am just sitting at home,
about to write my column—on Indonesia this week. I thought we'd
do a little bit about ataraxia and why maintaining tranquillity was
so important. This means a freedom from distress and worry and
emotional homeostasis . . .

Tuesday, 10 August, 10.03 a.m.
Jo: I didn't hate the idea of indifference to health woes (from Friday's
recording). I think that's what I have been trying to do. Like, it's
impossible not to be a bit sad and angry about it. But accepting
what's happening I think has been integral to maintaining calm.
It is all so beyond my control. Also I think being around other

sick people all the time makes it feel less unjust—I'm not better or more deserving of health than any of the other poor buggers.

Wednesday, 11 August, 11.58 a.m.
Brigid: Heeey, Jo. Hope you can get sun on your face today—the weather is good out there. Thought we would zoom out—we've been talking about some heavy stuff—and we'd go for something a bit lighter. And that thing is contemplation. The Stoics didn't invent it, but they used it a lot. All the major Stoics had a habit of journalling—they used it as a way of looking back on the day and assessing how they'd acted, rather than recording what other people had done to them. Say you and I had got in a dispute in the newsroom, some sort of fight. If you were a Stoic, in your journal that night you would write about yourself . . . you make an inventory of your own actions. You don't write about the other person, because you can't control their actions, so you just have to focus on yourself, what you did and how you could do better . . .

On it went, back and forth, this dialogue over WhatsApp, a way of connecting despite the barriers thrown up by our mutual isolation.

I found one of the strange joys of helping other people is that usually as a by-product, you end up helping yourself. As it was here, the Stoic voice notes that I sent to Jo throughout August and early September ended up clarifying to me the practical elements of Stoicism, such as the control test.

I had made a decision not to send Jo notes on death and grief. Her situation was too serious, and as you'll see later on, trying to apply the Stoic teachings on grief and death when you are deep in the weeds can be fraught.

But for Jo—in hospital, with cancer, during a pandemic—things such as the control test turned out to be very useful in helping her assess what she should and shouldn't worry about.

As winter turned into spring, and people began to emerge from their houses to picnic in small groups outside, I began to wonder how the philosophy could be applied not just to the big stuff but also to the smaller stuff. How could some of the daily issues that we face be solved if we were all a bit more Stoic? Might there be less anxiety? And what about the anger I saw increasing all around me (and occasionally from me)? Could there be less substance abuse? Could Stoicism assist in eradicating FOMO (the true scourge of the Instagram age)? And what about envy? And the lust for fame? And even disordered eating? Could something more than 2000 years old help with problems I thought of as being extremely modern?

Be calm

'Any person capable of angering you becomes your master; he can anger you only when you permit yourself to be disturbed by him.'

—Epictetus

'How much better to heal than seek revenge from injury. Vengeance wastes a lot of time and exposes you to many more injuries than the first that sparked it. Anger always outlasts hurt. Best to take the opposite course. Would anyone think it normal to return a kick to a mule or a bite to a dog?'

—Seneca

It was back in 2018, and we were driving to Denpasar airport in Indonesia. It was a nightmare. I saw almost three collisions, yet no one was honking their horn. There were hundreds of cars and motorbikes jammed into a terrible, potholed, narrow road yet the streets were actually kind of quiet.

'Where's all the road rage?' I asked my driver.

'What's road rage?' he asked.

Ha ha ha—*what's road rage?*

I gave him the sanitised version. 'It's this thing we have in Australia, where if you cut someone off, or don't let them into traffic or don't see them, or are driving too slowly—they will let you know by screaming at you, swearing at you, honking their horn, chasing you, trying to scare you, run you down, or kill you.'

'Er, no, people might get annoyed by other drivers but they are silent about it.'

I thought about the time a former colleague of mine was bashed and got his legs broken in Sydney after he yelled at a driver who almost ran over him at a pedestrian crossing. Being yelled at so incensed the driver that he got out of his car and beat the man to a pulp. My colleague was unable to walk for several months and had to use a wheelchair.

That's anger.

We got to Denpasar airport and the queues for departure were long. The couple behind me, Australians—were agitated and irritated. Aged maybe in their sixties, they were jostling, anxious and tetchy. They cursed the other queues that were moving faster, and the Indonesians who were checking passports too slowly. The husband was angry at the wife because she chose this SLOW QUEUE. Were they going to miss their flight? No—we were all on the same Melbourne-bound flight that would leave in a couple of hours. They stewed, fumed and sniped at each other. I felt tension radiating from them.

There is in all this—road rage, seething anger at queues or a fury at someone in your space—an enormous sense of entitlement. We demand that others not cause us discomfort. And if they cause us discomfort—even fleeting and minor discomfort by walking across our path—then some people spiral into a violent and seemingly unstoppable rage.

The rage has ripple effects too. The victim of the rage can react defensively and play into the drama by shouting or hitting back. Or they can take the shock and aggression with them, out into their day and snap or yell at others. The anger spread out, affecting so many others in a toxic ripple effect.

Yet we take for granted that people are angry. We are in an angry society, in an angry era. The last few years have been notable for increasingly high levels of rage—everywhere. Every day, anger is on display either in the home, in the street, on the roads or in the news.

In Bali, where I visit twice a year, I rarely see the locals get angry. My driver tells me this is because there is a strong culture in Indonesia of 'saving face'. It's incredibly bad form to lose control, start shouting at people, make a fuss and embarrass others in public. You only end up embarrassing yourself. But back on home soil, anger is never far from the surface. In Indonesia there might be anger expressed privately, but it's not so poorly contained as it is back in Australia.

In recent years, we've hit the accelerator on anger like never before; what was an extreme emotion is becoming normalised. It's on the streets, in the home, on our screens. There's no break from the anger. Instead, it just forms this sort of ambient background hum. According to the *Washington Post*, 'We're living, in effect, in a big anger incubator.'

This angry era went to the next level with the pandemic. After all, anger is a way of expressing fear and anxiety, and many of us have had a couple of years of feeling as if we are not in control anymore (although a Stoic will tell you this control you think you have lost was never yours to begin with).

With a lack of control comes fear, and with fear comes anger. Anger can be a way of saying 'enough'.

You may feel your anger is justified, that we are living in extraordinary times and that these extraordinary times require an extraordinary response.

But this is not true. According to the Stoics, anger is never justified.

Whatever form it takes, anger has terrible consequences both for you and others. But it is within your control to stop anger—and live a more tranquil and peaceful life.

Forgo the pleasure now to save pain later

'No plague has cost the human race more dearly than anger,' wrote Seneca nearly 2000 years ago.

In *De Ira* (*On Anger*), he offered therapeutic advice on how to prevent and control anger that is still highly applicable today.

On Anger is a nuanced work. After all, the Stoics also recognised that in releasing the poison of anger there is also an amount of pleasure in that release. This pleasure comes at a price though—mainly to your character, which can be deformed and corrupted by anger. Better to forgo the release, and not pay the larger cost down the line.

The Stoics believed that anger was a form of 'temporary madness' and did more harm to us than the event that we were trying to overcome.

When you have a flaky friend

Take the eternal problem of the bad friend. We've all had at least one—maybe we've even been one. It's the flaky friend who never calls you, rarely initiates social events and drops out of your life when you need her most. You become aware that it's been weeks since she called, and that the last four times it was you who made dinner arrangements and drove to her side of town. You feel like the friendship is unbalanced and unfair. You stew on this, getting more and more angry as the days go by. Meanwhile, she's oblivious to your pain. The anger builds. You get so angry and resentful of your friend that staying silent feels intolerable—you must let her know what you think!

But your anger about the situation is likely to cause far more harm to you than her neglect ever did. The consequences of getting angry at your friend—firing off an aggressive text for example, or shouting at her on the phone—is likely to make you feel good for a second or two, but guaranteed you'll hang up the phone and feel bad. With anger running the show, the conversation might also escalate—and she could or you could bring up all sorts of other past hurts and grievances. A minor problem (your friend being flaky) suddenly turns into a much bigger problem and you'll end up having to put more energy into repairing the friendship after you blew up than had you just calmly stated your needs and your hurt.

In fact, long after you've had the blow up and you've both stopped talking to each other—but you're both still hurt and fuming—you're likely to forget what the fight was about in the first place. This is what the Stoics referred to as 'suffering twice'. The first suffering is unavoidable: you have no control over whether your friend phones you or not—that is up to her. But the second suffering—your angry response, via a fight or email or even just nursing the angry feeling—is *within your control*. You are the only one to blame for that suffering. You chose it.

As Seneca asked: 'How does it help . . . to make troubles heavier by bemoaning them?'

So what should you do? The Stoic response to the situation is to not tackle it with your friend while you are angry. In fact you should avoid feeling angry in the first place. (We'll look at how to do that soon.) You can also try to persuade your friend to behave differently, but do not expect that she will.

So why do we get so angry?

Aristotle—who pre-dated the Greek Stoics by a few decades—believed that the reason for anger is to repay suffering. He believed that anger is one of the most complex human emotions and that it can be both a dangerous force that disrupts the social order and also a means of expressing discontent and desire for revenge when an injustice is done. He believed these two things need to be weighed up and anger must be doled out only rarely. He said, 'Anybody can become angry, that is easy; but to be angry with the right person, and to the right degree, and at the right time, and for the right purpose, and in the right way, that is not within everybody's power and is not easy.'

The Stoics were less measured about anger and believed that, in its raw, primal form, it had no place. Instead unrealistic expectations about the world are at the root of anger.

Much of Stoic teachings around anger are around how to control it.

You may say, 'That's all well and good to tell me that anger is bad, but it comes on so quickly that I don't have time to control it.'

Or you might say, 'Yes, I recognise anger is bad but, when I've been wronged, it can feel great to express anger.'

Or you might say, 'How am I meant to tackle injustice and all the problems in the world, if I numb my anger?'

All these questions preoccupied the Stoics, who in many ways were in an age just as angry as our own.

When Seneca wrote *On Anger*, he had already been plagued by significant health problems that required a lengthy convalescence in

Egypt, he'd fallen foul of the emperor Caligula and been banished from Rome to Corsica (after having to plead for his life to be spared on the grounds that ill health was likely to kill him anyway) and he'd been (perhaps falsely) charged with adultery. He had reason to be angry but fought against these impulses using reason and virtue.

In *On Anger*, Seneca acted as a philosopher/physician, diagnosing the problem (anger) and then providing the remedies. These remedies still hold up today.

It is not in our nature to be angry

The Stoics believed our nature as humans is fundamentally good and that we are social and communal beings who are meant to live together harmoniously. (As Marcus Aurelius wrote, 'people exist for one another'.)

Anger—with its assertion of individual rights and entitlements—breaks this social contract.

Seneca, expanding on this notion, wrote: 'Mankind is born for mutual assistance, anger for mutual ruin: the former loves society, the latter estrangement. The one loves to do good, the other to do harm; the one to help even strangers, the other to attack even its dearest friends. The one is ready even to sacrifice itself for the good of others, the other to plunge into peril provided it drags others with it.'

So what to do when someone makes us angry? It's simple really. Seneca said, 'We are bad men living among bad men; and only one thing can calm us—we must agree to go easy on one other.'

That one sentence—'we must agree to go easy on each other'—points to a mutual accord. We all put down our weapons, *go easy on each other* and not get riled up in the first place.

And in today's anger incubator, where everything seems to escalate so quickly and cool heads are hard to find—now, more than ever, we must chill.

So how do we control our anger?

You might argue 'expressing anger feels good—so it must be natural'.

The natural-seeming part of anger comes from legitimate feelings: that one has been wronged, or that someone we loved has been wronged, or that we are vulnerable to being hurt, or that we are suffering. What is road rage or anger at a bad driver but a manifestation of this feeling that the bad driver might have killed or hurt you, that you are scared and vulnerable in his path?

That release comes at enormous cost—it destroys your tranquillity and damages your character. Better to forgo the release—and not pay the larger cost down the line.

So how do you forgo the release?

Unsurprisingly, the Stoics had systematised a response to anger so that students could learn how to respond to situations calmly and using their rational mind.

Resist anger from the very beginning

Strike quickly, advised Seneca. As soon as you feel anger coming on you need to fight it. He wrote:

> The best plan is to reject straightway the first incentives to anger, to resist its very beginnings, and to take care not to be betrayed into it: for if once it begins to carry us away, it is hard to get back again into a healthy condition, because reason goes for

nothing when once passion has been admitted to the mind, and has by our own free will been given a certain authority, it will for the future do as much as it chooses, not only as much as you will allow it. The enemy, I repeat, must be met and driven back at the outermost frontier-line: for when he has once entered the city and passed its gates, he will not allow his prisoners to set bounds to his victory.

Check your emotional response

So how do you stop yourself from reacting to an insult or aggressive behaviour without getting angry? By keeping check of your emotional reaction. As we discussed in the previous chapter, there are two major forms of emotion: those arising from what the Stoics called 'impressions', and those arising from our judgements.

Keeping control over your emotions is hard. When someone attacks you, the effort to resist the attack can feel almost superhuman. But, like working a muscle, it is possible to control your anger (and all your emotions) through consciousness. You become conscious when an emotion arises (often you can feel it arising in your body in the form of tension or a contraction) and ask yourself if it's an impression—so an almost unconscious physiological reaction to something, like jumping when you are startled. Or is your emotion the product of a judgement? It's the product of a judgement when you label something good or bad.

By not attaching an emotion or judgement to an issue or stalling or changing a judgement, you are changing or adjusting your perception of the issue. All this is within your power, as long as you are aware and examine the judgement you are applying to a situation.

('Thinking is difficult, that's why people judge,' said psychoanalyst Carl Jung.)

Stalling making a judgement is a cognitive trick; you just slow down your thinking so you become more aware of what judgements you make.

You'll remember Chrysippus likened emotions to running too fast. The idea was to slow down your emotions—or at least become conscious of them as they are arising—and in slowing them, recasting or reconfiguring your judgement.

Said Marcus Aurelius, 'Get rid of this, make a decision to quit thinking of things as insulting, and your anger immediately disappears. How do you get rid of these thoughts? By realising that you've not really been harmed by their actions.'

Ask yourself—have I been harmed?

I have a nemesis on Twitter. I provoke anger in her. We've never met, but almost every time I tweet something whimsical, she gets furious and sends me provocative and angry replies, accusing me of being stupid, or tone deaf or privileged. I am always tempted to rise to the bait, but what I don't like in her, I don't want to see in myself. So I just let her tweet what she wants about me (I cannot control her; I can only control my reaction) and I remember Marcus Aurelius's advice: 'Get rid of this, make a decision to quit thinking of things as insulting, and your anger immediately disappears.'

I also remember the Stoic lessons on mortality and time. We are dying every day and time is precious. To get caught in a stupid feud or in an unresolvable, endless exchange with a stranger on the internet is to be wasting precious time.

The control test and anger

When dealing with anger, bring in the control test. Remember: work out what you can control and focus on those areas, rather than trying to control things outside your realm. It's when we have a false sense of how much we can control that we become frustrated and angry because we are scared (either unconsciously or consciously) by our lack of control. We could get angry at a driver on the road who drifted into our lane. They have long sped off, but we are still angry and triggered, even though we cannot do anything about it and the driver is gone.

Or it could be anger that is a more disguised form of fear. Say there are job losses at your company; scared, you become increasingly controlling at work, terrible at collaborating, hoarding projects, or not sharing or not being consultative because deep down you are frightened that you may lose your job. Anger takes many different forms including controlling behaviour, violence, bullying and needing to be right all the time.

Another example is becoming angry at the politics of another country. Take the US presidential election of 2016. The results caused a lot of anger in progressive circles, but for someone who wasn't American, and didn't have a vote in that country, I spent a hell of a lot of the years Trump was in office getting angry. I got angry when I read Twitter; I got angry when I saw his rallies on the news; I got angry reading articles about Trump; I got angry at his policies. Over the four years I spent probably hundreds of hours and expended huge amounts of energy on something that I could not control: I couldn't vote him out. I worked myself up into a lather when my time could have been spent more productively, working on causes in my own country.

Ask yourself: am I getting angry about something that I can change and is in my control?

If so, that is not a green light to get angry. Nothing is. But it is signalling that you can try to engage with something in a productive way.

Remember, there are only three things you can control:

- your character
- how you treat others
- your actions and reactions.

Dealing with anger

Express yourself

Avoiding anger doesn't mean that you are passive. Instead you can assert yourself and your principles in a way that gets a message across but doesn't disturb your tranquillity. For example, a few years ago when I was living in Melbourne my roof started leaking. The apartment above had a faulty radiator and water was dripping into my apartment. It was a Sunday and my neighbour seemed reluctant to pay a call-out fee for a plumber. She appeared to have little regard for the fact that my roof was at risk of caving in and said she would call a plumber in the morning. I felt angry at her lack of concern for my apartment. A sensation rose up in my body that felt like heat. When talking to her, I felt my breathing become shallow and anger come on. But instead of expressing it in a burst of rage, I let it pass and then spoke to her firmly and politely instead, insisting she call a plumber, after explaining what the consequences were for my apartment. Taking a firm tone and explaining consequences was enough to spur my neighbour into action. It didn't need to descend into shouting or insults, which would have poisoned an otherwise neutral relationship and made my neighbour potentially defensive and uncooperative, and perhaps even turned her into an enemy.

Beware of emotion that starts with anger that goes unexpressed in a relationship. It can show up as nagging, passive aggression, resentment, self-pity, sulking or punishing the other person in a myriad of ways. Instead, wait until the heat of your anger has cooled, then express your feelings in a rational manner.

GUILT AND SHAME

Anger directed at oneself can become guilt or shame. Stoicism had no use for these emotions (they became popular later on with the rise of Christianity). The Stoic view on character was clear. You are in control of your character. There is no value in shame—if your character is deficient, work hard to change it and let the virtues be your guide.

As Marcus Aurelius said, 'Waste no more time arguing what a good man should be. Be one.' Be a good woman also. Or just a good person.

Avoiding social media

Stoics saw anger as contagious, meaning that someone else's anger could infect you if it spread in a mob-like setting. And the place where mobs congregate today? The internet. More specifically, social media.

Stoics of course did not have to deal with social media but they were social beings who thought deeply about how the mob could incite high emotions such as anger. (They would have been fascinated by a tool that allowed the whole world to talk to one another.) They were highly aware of the importance of not falling prey to the contagion. Philosophers were often the victims—for example, jurors put Socrates to death by hemlock poisoning in 399 BC, for 'corrupting the young'.

We can't control other people's anger, but we can definitely control our own.

One of the positive steps we can take in managing our own anger is to disengage from social media that encourages the amplification of anger. Twitter and Facebook are the two most toxic platforms in this regard. People spend all day engaged in petty disputes on the internet, often in the name of social justice or some cause they align with but they don't realise the 'work' they do on social media just enriches the platform and has very little impact in the real world outside their particular timeline. (Even then, has anyone ever backed down from an opinion on Twitter because they were persuaded to take a different view? Rarely.)

Don't be soft

Seneca believed that if we are too sensitive, coddled or protected we can become quick to anger because we have an overdeveloped sense of entitlement or are used to deference or excessive comfort.

Many things will seem unbearable to us because we are not sufficiently hardened up. We may be angered by what Seneca called 'vulgar trivialities' such as a lukewarm drink or a meal at a restaurant that is not to our liking and fly into a rage at the waitstaff.

Seneca warned against 'anger [that] lasts longer than the damage done to us' (i.e. the damage done by a meal that is not hot enough) and said we are less likely to get angry if we lose our sense of entitlement and become comfortable with discomfort.

The more we are used to discomfort (see the chapter 'How to Cope with Disaster'), the less rattled and angry we'll be when things aren't 100 per cent smooth or perfect.

The Stoics in their teachings had several practical exercises for their students to undertake to make them used to this discomfort. These include trying to adapt our bodies and brains to uncomfortable situations. This might include not wearing shoes and walking on a hot or very cold road, not wearing a jumper when it's chilly outside, not carrying an umbrella, sleeping on the floor or eating simple and plain food at a lukewarm temperature.

What the Stoics were essentially talking about is cultivating resilience.

This resilience then protected the Stoics when worse things happened. When the Stoic philosopher Musonius Rufus was banished by Emperor Nero, he said 'an exiled person is not prevented from having virtue, courage, self-control or wisdom'. Rather than getting angry at being exiled, he saw the benefits. Not only was he able to exercise his virtues but exile doubled as a health retreat: 'Other people whose bodies have been ruined by luxurious living, regained their health as a result of being banished,' he said.

Modern Stoic William Irvine believes that in modern times people have been treated as less than capable by politicians and psychologists. 'A resilient person will refuse to play the role of victim . . . She may not be able to control whether she is the target of injustice but she has considerable control over how she responds to being targeted. She can let it ruin her day or her life—or she can look for ways around the obstacles.'

This person doesn't waste her time being angry and stewing about her injustice—instead she sees what can be salvaged out of the situation.

Don't be curious about what people are saying about you

Avoid being curious about your reputation, as you may find out something that will ignite your anger, counselled Seneca in *On Anger*. This advice has aged well and could be read as warning about the dangers of googling yourself, or searching for your name on Twitter. No good will come of it, and your tranquillity is bound to be disturbed.

'It does not serve one's interest to see everything, or to hear everything. Many offences may slip past us, and most fail to strike home when a man is unaware of them,' Seneca wrote. 'Do you want to avoid losing your temper? Resist the impulse to be curious. The man who tries to find out what has been said against him, who seeks to unearth spiteful gossip, even when engaged privately, is destroying his own peace of mind. Certain words can be construed in such a way that they appear insulting . . .'

Don't look at your partner's phone or emails, even if you have an excellent, trusting relationship. You are sure to find something to disturb you—and something that also will be easy to misinterpret—if you look hard enough. Remember the importance of keeping a tranquil mind.

Delay, delay, delay

Seneca said, 'The greatest cure for anger is to wait, so that the initial passion it engenders may die down, and the fog that shrouds the mind may subside, or become less thick.'

This age-old technique of delay works. You just have to not let the emotion take over and words spill out faster than your rational mind can keep up. You need to put the brakes on.

So . . . take a few deep breaths if you can physically feel yourself getting angry (you'll know because your heart will start racing, your pulse will increase, you may feel your face start to flush or your breath to feel constricted). These few seconds of pause are crucial in giving yourself some space for your rational mind to catch up with your emotions.

As well as a few deep breaths you could also physically leave the room, hang up the phone (after you've explained that you are feeling too emotional to continue the conversation) or reply to a text or an email that has angered you but put it in your drafts folder.

You are buying yourself precious time to let your emotions cool and find a way out of the interaction that will not damage you or the other person down the line.

If the physical feeling of the anger threatens to overwhelm you, just remind yourself that even the most intense and strong sensations of anger will quickly pass.

Said Seneca: 'Some of the affronts that were sweeping you off your feet will lose their edge in an hour, not just in a day, others will disappear altogether; if the delay you sought produces no effect, it will be clear that judgement now rules, not anger. If you want to determine the nature of anything, entrust it to time: when the sea is stormy, you can see nothing clearly.'

Use the energy of anger without getting angry

There is a lot of energy in anger, so it may feel good, because previously we might have felt apathetic or stuck. A burst of heat can have a remarkable cleansing effect, like a firestorm coming through a dense forest. Of course, as we know, what feels cleansing at the time can have dire consequences. Instead the trick is to use the energy of anger in a positive way.

We can use the energy of anger to create change and spur us on and out of an unhealthy situation or a toxic relationship but we don't actually have to explode with anger at the other person. Instead we use the sensations or feeling of anger to give us a cue that things might need to change in our own lives. Anger then becomes a form of intuition or a guide. We can feel the anger, but then use the techniques that Seneca recommended such as delay, to not be reactive. But the initial strong feeling—once examined in the cool light of day by our rational mind—might provide clues about where we are dissatisfied, frustrated or need a change. Not being angry is *not* the same as putting up with bullshit. The angry impulse contains important messages. The initial angry feeling may point to actions we need to take such as removing ourselves from a situation or person, ending a relationship, changing jobs or moving teams. It could also stimulate a greater engagement with social justice issues if we find ourselves getting angry at a failure in the system or with the status quo (the Black Lives Matter and #MeToo protests are a prime example of where anger at the status quo can be used as fuel to fight for social change).

RIGHTEOUSNESS IS DANGEROUS

Anger can also contain an element of righteousness, which adds further fuel to the emotion. With righteousness, it becomes very important to show the other person that you are right and they are wrong.

Making the other person 'wrong' is a way of justifying our anger but, if you look at the situation from their perspective, most people actually never see their actions as wholly wrong. There is always probably, on their side, a justification for their actions. No one really sees themselves as the 'bad guy'—not even bad guys. Many will have a reason or justification for acting as they do, and, if you say they are wrong, they will be unlikely to see themselves as being in the wrong and will become defensive. In these entrenched positions, neither side is inclined to give ground and a stalemate develops. Marcus Aurelius counselled:

> If what they're doing is right, you've no reason to complain; and if it's not right, then it must have been involuntary and unintentional. Because just as 'no one ever deliberately denies the truth', according to Socrates, so few people ever intentionally treat another person badly. That's why these negative people are themselves insulted if anyone accuses them of injustice, ingratitude, meanness, or any other sort of offence against their neighbours, they just don't realise they're doing wrong.

Toxic masculinity

Marcus Aurelius wrote about anger a lot in his *Meditations*, because it was an issue he sought to control in his own life. He recognised that the sign of a 'real man' is not anger, but the ability to remain calm. The ability to remain calm requires greater strength and self-control than giving into the easy but destructive pleasures of blowing off some steam by taking out your rage and frustration onto others.

'Keep this thought handy when you feel a fit of rage coming on— it isn't manly to be enraged. Rather, gentleness and civility are more human, and therefore manlier. A real man doesn't give way to anger and discontent, and such a person has strength, courage, and endurance—unlike the angry and complaining. The nearer a man comes to a calm mind, the closer he is to strength,' he wrote.

Fake anger

Parents and teachers in particular know the benefits of pretending to be angry. It is used to send a message to people who might need guidance or discipline (such as children) but the person delivering the message must ensure their tranquillity is not disturbed. Feigning anger is a way of keeping your tranquillity and self-control intact while imparting a strong message. It might be that your child has taken off their seat belt while you are driving or a student is seriously disrupting a class by throwing things at other students. In these instances you need to deliver a message as effectively as possible. The behaviour is not to be tolerated. Fake anger can help in this respect. But it is not to be used when talking with a peer or a partner. Instead it is more likely to fuel their anger and lead to a situation being escalated.

Social justice

How do you square avoidance of anger with social change? That's a question I asked myself a lot as I was studying Stoicism.

In fact it was probably the main thing Andrew and I kept coming back to when we debated and discussed the merits of Stoicism. Both of us saw major weaknesses in Stoicism when it came to taking action to bring about greater social justice.

What use was eradicating anger if it made you completely passive and unable to agitate for social change? How to fight injustice if you were too busy cultivating tranquillity? It is the same charge levelled by some at Buddhism: that is, non-attachment means you might feel relaxed and at peace, but what about your duty to those around you? What about the part you must play in bringing about social change?

After two years of debating Stoicism and social change, we came to an understanding that the avoidance of anger and progressive politics didn't need to be mutually exclusive. In fact, you were more likely to be an effective agent of justice and change if you channelled Stoic techniques, including controlling anger. Controlling anger allows you to build consensus and alliances, and to communicate your position clearly and compellingly without becoming overwrought; having a rational mind allows you to plot a course of action so that change is achieved as peacefully and effectively as possible.

Ancient Stoics were heavily represented in politics. They believed that humans were social animals who were interdependent, and that all were equal—including men and women, and slaves and free people. These relatively progressive beliefs (for the time)—the prime belief that we are social beings, as well as the 'justice' being one of the major Stoic virtues—mean that social change is something that can be incorporated into Stoic philosophy.

A rational mind

As Marcus Aurelius said, 'The nearer a man comes to a calm mind, the closer he is to strength.'

One of the reasons that the Stoic took such pains to avoid anger was because it warped rationality. For example: you're at a football match, and someone doesn't watch where they are going; they step on your foot, then turn around and spill their drink on you, and then they don't even apologise! If you were thinking rationally, you might accept that it was an accident, wipe yourself off, note the lack of manners from the bystander, but then dismiss it because you can't control if other people are polite. You might never think of the incident again, and forgot it even happened five seconds after the encounter. But what if anger—or its even angrier cousin, rage—steps in to defend you and the suffering caused by the spilt drink and lack of apology? Rage will say 'how dare you do this to me, you klutz' (or much worse).

And now provoked, the spiller may become defensive and throw a whole beer on you, glass you in the face or hit you.

In this moment, your rational mind has been completely over-taken by an irrational surge of anger. You might be kicked out of the football match or end up in court. Your day—and maybe your life—would be ruined because you gave in to anger.

But you always had the choice to use what is always there: your rationality.

You can also be annoying

Marcus Aurelius also had to remind himself that it is futile to 'other' or demonise someone who has angered you, because, if your fellow human has made a mistake or acted in an inflammatory manner, then you probably have too.

'You yourself, are no different from them, and upset people in various ways,' he wrote. This is a great lesson in not taking the moral high road. Even if you do control your anger, realise that you can be annoying to other people, just as other people can be annoying to you. When this happens, we do as Seneca suggested and 'Agree to go easy on each other'.

Be moderate

'And as long as nothing satisfies you, you yourself cannot satisfy others.'   —Seneca

'Eat merely to relieve your hunger; drink merely to quench your thirst; dress merely to keep out the cold; house yourself merely as a protection against personal discomfort.'   —Seneca

My relationship with alcohol has been long and strong. I've had some good nights, followed by some very ordinary days (shades drawn, a full fat can of Coke beading on the bedside table, the dull pop of the blister pack of Panadol) trying to sleep away that woozy, drained feeling.

Until recently I had merrily lived according to Winston Churchill's maxim: 'I have taken more good from alcohol than alcohol has taken from me.'

But now alcohol is subtracting good with abandon.

Recently I was sitting in my friend Susie's backyard, incredibly grouchy because I had had only four hours of broken sleep the night before.

'I don't get it; I didn't even drink that much and I woke up in the middle of the night—2.23 a.m. to be precise!—and couldn't get back to sleep. It felt like I was digesting a brick.'

It had been happening a lot lately. Alcohol was breaking me. After even a small amount, the next day I felt ready for rehab.

I always thought my break-up with alcohol would happen after I'd been arrested or said something terrible to someone important or fallen down a flight of stairs, but the reality was turning out to be more prosaic. I just couldn't process alcohol in the way I used to. I'd wake up at strange hours. I'd feel sick. After drinks on Friday, I'd have hangovers that lasted until Wednesday. It was like my body, after years of enjoying drinking, had just . . . stopped.

The shift had been so abrupt that I began to wonder if each person is allocated a number of drinks to consume over a lifetime and I had used up all my rations before I'd used up my years.

'We need to find something new,' said Susie. 'So I've been thinking . . . nangs.'

'Nangs?'

'Yes, nangs.'

Nangs are what teenagers around Bondi inhale after dark in public parks. On my beach walks I would find the empty canisters littered under trees in clusters. But we had missed the party by decades.

'No, we're not doing nangs,' I said. I searched my mind for the next reliable (or perhaps reliably unreliable) dopamine high that would lift my spirits without wrecking my body. Nothing came to mind, except for perhaps micro-dosing or light beer. Nothing except for perhaps . . . moderation? Maybe I could enjoy the things I used to enjoy in large quantities, in much smaller quantities.

Moderation, moderation . . . I rolled the unfamiliar word around on my tongue. Maybe moderation was the answer. But how the hell would I do it?

Like almost *everyone* I know, I was brought up in a binge-drinking culture. My teen years growing up in a country, coastal town were an exhilarating blur of parties when the parents were away, sickly green Midori in a paddock on someone's farm under the wash of the Milky Way, the first sip of bourbon on the playground equipment down by the railway tracks, sweet vermouth from a parental liquor cabinet, port mixed with Mellow Yellow down at the caravan park, hot summers' nights down at the beach that felt like heaven and smelt like salt air and sea grass.

Then college. Next level. Drinking games and rituals from the moment we stepped into the quadrangle on that hot February day, the air heavy with the scent of eucalyptus. Three years passed in a blur of formal dinners, cheap port, voluminous quantities of beer, hung-over days of missed classes—late for lunch, leaning in on those large, round tables to share the gossip from the night before.

Then a law firm in the country. People drank a lot. Thursday and Friday nights were spent at the rough local pub down by the port where the cops and the criminals and the lawyers all went to blow off steam.

Then journalism. The Sydney years. Wanted an in with the hardened police reporters, the clubby photographers, the overworked section editors? When you were young and had no currency to trade with senior colleagues, you could always buy them a drink and listen to their stories down at the pub.

The years passed. And passed. And passed some more.

I thought down the track someone would tap me on the shoulder, draw me into a hushed, neutrally toned room (their Moderation Diploma hanging on the wall) and sit me down and say, 'You are now at an age and stage in your life where you need to be more moderate. This is how it's done.'

That day never came. The indoctrination, the lengthy apprenticeship and schooling I had with binge drinking (and I passed! I passed all the binge-drinking exams with flying colours!!) never arrived for moderation.

No one ever told me: 'This is what moderation looks like.'

Of course, you could rightly say, 'You dill!! You don't need to be told! You just slow down! Stop having all the drinks! And stop eating whatever you want to eat, whenever you want to eat it!'

But moderation is easier said than done. What's more, it's never really marketed at us. Unlike a diet where you do an abrupt volte-face and completely change your regime (no carbs!, no sugar!, no dairy!, vegan!, juicing!) and get fast results that satisfy the need for immediate gratification, moderation is low and slow. It's not part of the capitalistic industrial wellness complex and therefore not pushed in our face over and over and over again, until seduced—or ground down—we hand over our credit card for a course of moderation.

In the years since the Chinese herb fast, where I had dramatic weight loss (and then the subsequent gain), I have been on a number of enthusiastic but short-lived health kicks that all left me out of pocket but failed to provide sustainable results.

They included a personal training gym—where I saw a trainer *every day*—a keto fast supervised by a nutritionist where I ate one high fat meal a day and nothing else, and an app where I had to laboriously calculate the macronutrients of everything I put in my mouth.

But what if I gave moderation a go? Boring, plodding, unsexy, sensible moderation?

Because there was someone around to teach me moderation. There were a lot of people, in fact (even though they were all dead). They were of course the Stoics, who saw moderation as so central to their way of life that they made it a virtue and called it temperance. They labelled pleasure—including drinking alcohol and enjoying fancy food—as a preferred indifferent.

Why did they do that?

The Roman Stoics lived in a time not dissimilar to ours when it came to hedonism, abundance and excess. The Romans loved to get lit! As a result the Stoics thought and wrote a great deal about how to resist temptations and practise moderation. Exotic foods—wild fruits, honey, rare game, ice and exciting spices—were sourced from across the empire, and made their way to the capital in an old-fashioned version of air-miles. Alcohol and food in particular took up a lot of unpaid rent in the Stoics' heads. Some of Stoicism's most enduring lessons are around moderation.

But before I start, there is a caveat around moderation, which is that not everyone can moderate. This is not a character flaw but is down to a complicated range of factors, including environmental factors, brain chemistry and propensity for addiction that would not have been understood by Stoics at the time. Some people lack an 'off switch' when it comes to drinking (or other addictive behaviours), where according to the old AA adage: 'one drink is too many and a thousand is not enough'. For this group of people, moderation is difficult, if not impossible—and the best path (I'm talking alcohol here) is abstinence.

Out of all the four Stoic virtues, moderation (or temperance) is the most modest-sounding and achievable. But it proved, for me at least, one of the hardest to master. Courage is often reactive and instinctive, coming on in spurts depending on the circumstances, propelling you onto the train tracks to rescue the baby, or plunging into the surf to grab a drowning tourist. Wisdom accretes slowly, usually with the years; although it can be hard won, it's a muscle that builds over time until it becomes second nature. It doesn't require enormous daily willpower to be wise. Justice springs from nature (the concept of natural justice, still taught in law schools today, has its roots in Stoic principles) and we can recognise it and exercise it by tuning in. Also, again, no willpower needed.

But moderation? This seemingly slight virtue is the toughest to master. The work never stops! In being moderate we must resist all the siren songs of abundance that are everywhere in today's world, as they were in Roman society. We must ignore our eyes that see the heaped plate of tempting and delicious food, and ignore our rumbling stomach, and we must ignore the heavenly smells and the involuntary physiological responses including the stimulation of saliva glands (the drool, the watering mouth), and refuse the hostess already piling our plates high with meats and treats. We must place a hand over the glass to stop the pour of the generous friend, and we must instead, as Epictetus advised, 'put out your hand, and take a moderate share'. And we must do it day after day after day, meal after meal after meal.

It is not just in relation to food and drink where moderation is virtue. The virtue of temperance can be extended to all addictive or more-ish habits: social media, drugs, television, the internet . . . Moderate, moderate, moderate.

Why is moderation important?

Have too much of anything and your body will make a complaint; you'll feel ill or slightly off or knocked out of balance. Think about when you overdo it on the chocolate or eat a whole bag of corn chips in one sitting. It may feel good at the time but, when you snap out of your fugue state, look at the empty wrappers and then check in with your body to see how you're feeling, you're not going to feel great. There are both the physical feeling of being too full and the psychological feelings of guilt, shame and regret.

Yet somehow we don't learn.

Take drinking alcohol, for example. It would be enough to have one big, messy night and then wake up in pain. Head hanging over the toilet bowl the next morning, we vow 'never again' but often this promise is long forgotten by the following Friday night and the situation is repeated. This can go on for years, with the body and its organs slowly being worn down by regular overindulgence.

We can take corrective measures but they can also be too extreme. I have deprived myself completely of things before, but in an echo of the excesses described elsewhere in this book, I have balanced the deprivation with hedonistic binges in order to achieve a deranged sort of homeostasis (but homeostasis nonetheless). Existing in such extreme states takes its toll on the body. But to moderate is perhaps to be in a continual or near-enough continual state of homeostasis without having to rely on extreme states to achieve balance. As a result, the body and mind themselves are not disturbed by having to deal with too much or too little, and tranquillity is a natural by-product.

Modern Stoic Donald Robertson has written on Medium about how to eat and drink like a Stoic. One of Robertson's main inspirations for his Medium article is Musonius Rufus, who had many opinions about food. Wrote Robertson:

> Musonius taught that Stoics should prefer *inexpensive* foods that are easy to obtain and most nourishing and healthy for a human being to eat. It might seem like common sense to 'eat healthy' but the Stoics also thought we potentially waste far too much time shopping for and preparing fancy meals when simple nutritious meals can often be easily prepared from a few readily available ingredients.
>
> Musonius advises eating plants and grains rather than slaughtered animals. He recommends fruits and vegetables that do not require much cooking, as well as cheese, milk, and honeycombs.

The Stoics weren't strict vegetarians but they didn't eat a lot of meat, either.

These were other Stoic food and drink habits highlighted by Robertson:

- avoiding gourmet food
- eating slowly and mindfully
- choosing nutritious food over sweet food (so fruit instead of lollies), strengthening the body rather than pleasing the palate
- sharing food—and not taking a larger portion than is needed.

Fasting was also adopted by the Stoic community and, as you know from the chapter 'How to Cope with Disaster', going without food is an important Stoic lesson in training the body and the mind for potential deprivation or change in circumstances down the line (towards the end of his life, Seneca ate very little—preferring figs and fruit from his estate).

The Stoics believed moderation was the key to feeling, thinking and looking good. They saw it wasn't just good for avoiding hangovers and overeating, but that the practice of moderation flowed into a range of other areas and behaviours. Be moderate with food and drink and then, with the exercise of your self-control muscles, you'll find moderation spreads to other areas of your life that might be unruly or unbalanced one way or the other—such as the propensity to do anything too much, whether that be work, sport, eating or sleeping.

Roman Stoic Musonius Rufus wrote that the beginning and foundation of temperance lay in self-control in eating and drinking, and how moderation was a good practise for exercising self-control in other areas of life. 'If we were to measure what is good by how much pleasure it brings, nothing would be better than self-control, if we were to measure what is to be avoided by its pain, nothing would be more painful than lack of self-control,' he wrote.

How much is enough?

If you asked a Stoic what moderation entails, they would say you must consume enough to live and be healthy, but not more than you need. 'Enough' is consuming what is necessary to relieve the physical discomfort of hunger and to give the body strength to do what it needs to do throughout the day. It's an eat-to-live thing, rather than live to eat.

Seneca wrote: 'Hold fast, then, to this sound and wholesome rule of life, that you indulge the body only so far as is needful for good health. The body should be treated more rigorously, so that it may not be disobedient to the mind. Eat merely to relieve your hunger; drink merely to quench your thirst; dress merely to keep out the cold; house yourself merely as a protection against personal discomfort.'

What he meant by this was eat and drink enough to satisfy hunger and thirst but be rigorous and don't oversaturate it with too much fuel. This is very similar to the Japanese concept of *hara hachi bun me*. It means 'eat until you're 80 per cent full'. It originated with Confucius and is still followed in the city of Okinawa, where people use this advice as a way to control their eating habits. Interestingly, Okinawa has one of the lowest rates of illness from heart disease, cancer and stroke, and is famous for its elders living past 100.

Addiction can destroy rationality

The virtue of moderation has so much more to recommend it than just a good feeling—or balance—in your body. Not overindulging also allows you to think clearly, see the world clearly, make rational decisions and not be enslaved to appetites or desires that will need to be sated over and over and over again (aka addiction). Moderation is a way of taking your power back from an outside source or force that might have been difficult to control.

The cycle of overindulgence followed by regret is not just confusing for the body (and often counterproductive to goals such as weight loss) but it can disturb the mind and lead to addictions and attachments.

As addiction can compromise rational thought, a Stoic would advise that you avoid all addictions.

Seneca wrote of the loss of rationality that comes from drinking too much, 'Cruelty usually follows wine-bibbing; for a man's soundness of mind is corrupted and made savage. Just as a lingering illness makes men querulous and irritable and drives them wild at the least crossing of their desires, so continued bouts of drunkenness besti-alise the soul.'

The Stoics were not the first to preach moderation. A carving on the front of the temple at Delphi reads 'Nothing in excess', while Socrates taught that a man must know 'how to choose the mean and avoid the extremes on either side, as far as possible'.

The influential Greek philosopher Aristotle, who pre-dated the Stoics (and who had been taught by Plato, who in turn had been a student of Socrates), set out his principles for moderation under the banner of the 'golden mean'. The golden mean is between two states of extremity and deprivation. The extreme of courage is recklessness and at the other end is cowardice. The wise person lives in the middle.

The benefits of moderation—or a version of the golden mean—can also be found in the foundations of Taoism. Moderation in Taoism is not just a desirable behaviour, but a spiritual practice. 'Pounding an edge to sharpness/Will not make it last,' says the Tao Te Ching.

Moderation can keep you tranquil

People spend their whole lives, often unconsciously, swinging from one extreme state to the other, from binging to purging, from overindulgence to complete abstinence. They love the drama! But if we have tranquillity as one of the major ingredients for having a good life, this will be disrupted by swinging between these extremes. How can you be tranquil when you are either in the depths of a hangover, full of anxiety about what you said the night before, or feeling agitated and deprived as you say no to a glass of champagne at a celebration or a piece of cake on your birthday?

I've fallen into the trap—as have many—of enjoying something, whether it be a drink or delicious food, but I'm actually thinking about what I'm going to have next, even while I still have something in my mouth! My mind races ahead. I like coffee so much, I'll be planning when to have my second coffee while I'm still drinking my first.

Moderation, self-control, temperance—whatever you want to call it—is the ideal condition for tranquillity to flourish. You're not constantly distracted by wanting *more*.

Moderation when it comes to food and drink is *not* the same as abstinence. Instead it might mean having one drink or one small piece of cake rather than having so much alcohol that you feel unstable, unsteady and out of control, or so much food that you feel sick or uncomfortable.

Notice how much of your life force, your energy and focus, playfulness and attention is thrown off balance when you either indulge too much or deprive yourself for too long.

A Stoic guide to boozing

Getting drunk, trying not to get drunk, limiting their drinking, having alcohol-free days, trying to keep their wits about them, devising rules and exceptions to those rules about drinking—all of it very much occupied the ancient Stoics. Someone should write a book called 'Ancients, they're just like us!'

Ancient Stoics thought a lot about drinking, and how too much of it could violate some of their rules for life. Reliance on alcohol and other drugs can lead to addiction, which impairs not only rationality and self-control (as we have discussed), but can also degrade character.

So how did the ancient Stoics drink?

According to Donald Robertson, 'The historian Diogenes Laertius, a "doxographer" who recorded the views of Greek philosophers, says that the Stoics typically drank wine in *moderation*, but would not allow themselves to get drunk. Stobaeus, another doxographer, tells us that the Stoics classified excessive love of wine as a disease, although curiously they considered *hating* it too much to be one as well.'

Because controlling alcohol use is an age-old, very common and *very human* problem, the Stoics devised some hacks to help with moderation.

Practise saying no

To practise moderation—say with drinking alcohol—there is an excellent ancient Stoic technique, which involves saying no to a glass of wine if it's offered to you, as a way of training yourself to master your desire for the thing that you crave.

Epictetus also encouraged students not to be grasping when it came to being offered food or drink. He used the example of the banquet in an analogy of the benefits of moderation—not just for food, but in life:

> Remember that you must behave as at a banquet. Is anything brought round to you? Put out your hand, and take a moderate share. Does it pass you? Do not stop it. Has it not come yet? Do not yearn in desire towards it, but wait till it reaches you. So with

regard to children, wife, office, riches; and you will some time or other be worthy to feast with the gods. And if you do not so much as take the things which are set before you, but are able even to forgo them, then you will not only be worthy to feast with the gods, but to rule with them also.

But there is a further element to Epictetus's teachings about wine. That is—if you are off the booze—don't brag about it.

'When someone drinks water alone, or adopts some other ascetic practice, he seizes every opportunity to tell everyone, "I drink nothing but water." . . . Man, if it brings you any benefit to drink it, then drink it; otherwise you're acting in a ridiculous fashion,' said Epictetus.

Ha ha ha. Epictetus was obviously wise to a truism throughout the ages—the only thing almost as bad as a drunk bore, is someone who bores you about *not drinking*.

So drink the water, exercise self-control, but for godsakes—don't go on about it.

WHY IS MODERATION SO IMPORTANT FOR THE PLANET?

It's not just our bodies that can benefit from moderation—the planet can too.

A few years ago I was up in the Kimberley in northern Australia, staying with one of the traditional owners, Bruno Dann. One morning we went down to the river to catch our dinner. The mud crabs were practically jumping out of the river. We caught several easily and left with enough for one for each person. But my greedy, Western mind was puzzled. 'Why don't we get more, Bruno?' I asked. 'We could have the rest later.'

The whole idea of taking more than we needed was an anathema to him. He explained that the only reason we were able to get mud crabs that day was because people who had been there before had only taken what they needed for themselves and not brought in an icebox or an esky to 'stock up'. Nature, he said, will provide if you don't get greedy and strip her of resources.

Traditional cultures knew this—understanding that nature was a finite resource and if you were greedy or immoderate then others would miss out—and eventually you would miss out too.

Bruce Pascoe in *Dark Emu* wrote, 'If we are to attempt to understand Indigenous philosophy it has to begin with the profound obligation to land.'

Moderation at both this personal and collective level is the natural way of things. Nature thrives when things are in balance—when we take just enough, what we need—and no more.

Remind yourself what good food and drink really *is*

Do you read a wine column or go to a cellar door on a vineyard tour and get carried away with the evocative descriptions of the wine? Do you walk away with a case of pinot noir because it sounded and tasted almost like poetry?

Marcus Aurelius rather brutally reminded us that fine wines are just mouldy grapes, delicious meats are the corpses of animals, and sex is just friction and motion.

How good it is when you have roast meat or suchlike foods before you, to impress on your mind that this is the dead body of a fish, this is the dead body of a bird or pig; and again, that the Falernian wine is the mere juice of grapes, and your purple edged robe simply the hair of a sheep soaked in shell-fish blood! And in sexual intercourse that it is no more than the friction of a membrane and a spurt of mucus ejected. How good these perceptions are at getting to the heart of the real thing and penetrating through it, so you can see it for what it is! This should be your practice throughout your life: when things have such a plausible appearance, show them naked, see their shoddiness, strip away their own boastful account of themselves.

If we reframe the things that we gorge on or indulge in, as cooked animal carcasses, for example, then they become less appealing to us.

In our culture, rich, fine food is heavily marketed as desirable and it's a signal of status to eat at high-end restaurants. Likewise, alcohol companies market ethanol flavoured with sugar as a sophisticated and desirable product that is the gateway to fun, friendship, sex and glamour. Like Marcus Aurelius, you should see these substances for what they really are.

You can still drink and have fun

The Stoics were not against drinking per se, and copious amounts of wine were often served at banquets they held and attended. Ancient Romans drank wine daily, and Seneca was known as a great appreciator of fine wine, and the owner of several large vineyards. (He was, after all, filthy rich.)

As social beings, Stoics believed it was important not to hide yourself away if others are drinking. Don't stay at home, watching all the fun on Instagram. You should still take part in festivals and celebrations, and enjoy yourself—just don't lose control. Join the party; just don't get off your head! Seneca advised: 'It shows much more courage to remain dry and sober when the mob is drunk and vomiting; but it shows greater self-control to refuse to withdraw oneself and to do what the crowd does, but in a different way, thus neither making oneself conspicuous nor becoming one of the crowd. For one may keep holiday without extravagance.'

And every once in a while get off your chops

There were exceptions to this 'mostly sober' rule, which to me make a lot of sense. They allow for lapses in self-control when the circumstances dictate. The Stoics saw that sometimes—I mean rarely—getting drunk could unlock something. Just think about times you've been in a slump and stuck in your own head. Maybe you've been dumped by your lover or lost your job. There's always a well-meaning friend who will try to get you out of your tracksuit, into something fancy and take you out for shots to 'drown your troubles'. They will say you need a jolt to the system. Sometimes a night out on the town can actually be the medicine you need to change into a different gear.

This is not so different from Stoic advice. Seneca thought, at times:

we ought to drink even to intoxication, not so as to drown, but merely to dip ourselves in wine, for wine washes away troubles and dislodges them from the depths of the mind and acts as a remedy to sorrow as it does to some diseases. The inventor of wine is called Liber, not from the licence which he gives to our tongues but because he liberates the mind from the bondage of cares and emancipates it, animates it and renders it more daring in all that it attempts.

While that sounds like the Stoics were having a bet each way, it's all in keeping with the rest of their philosophy. Moderation, self-control, discipline and then, once in a blue moon, if you need to cut loose, do it. It's about controlling your use of the substance, rather than the substance controlling you.

Be on social media

'I laugh at those who think they can damage me. They do not
know who I am, they do not know what I think, they cannot even
touch the things which are really mine and with which I live.'

—Epictetus

'I begin to speak only when I'm certain what I'll say isn't better
left unsaid.'
—Cato

O n my walks with Andrew, one of my regular complaints
was the beatings I would take on social media. It was—in
Stoic parlance—affecting my tranquillity. The social media
beatings would take several forms: someone tweeting bad things about
me and then people I know sending me screenshots of those tweets
(why? Why? It was the digital equivalent of handing me a freshly
produced dog turd and saying 'here—you might want to check this
out'); or my doing a tweet that was poorly worded, badly received and
misunderstood—and then suffering the shock of a sudden digital
pile-on (one stupid tweet I did was misinterpreted as calling for all

universities to be shut down; another—blaming Donald Trump for me not going to the gym and subsequently not having the strength to open jars—was the subject of a mocking segment on Fox News).

Andrew would shrug and remind me that other people's opinions came with the territory—the territory being that I had a weekly column with *The Guardian* that people were going to have views on. That was the territory but, now, with Stoicism, I had the map. I couldn't control what other people thought of me and, short of abandoning social media or abandoning my column, other people's opinions were out of my control.

Best to accept that heat on social media comes with the job and be more mindful of what I put out there—but also grow a thicker skin to shrug off the haters.

Gradually, that began to happen.

I have grown my Twitter followers but I take lengthy breaks away from the site by deactivating my account, and I use the mute button a lot if I think someone is going to rile me up. Best not to get involved and just use the platform to get news and media gossip, and promote my stories.

What is certain is that anyone using social media these days needs to have a plan around how they use it, and monitor not just the information they get on social media, but also their mood after spending too long online.

Social media feeds on strong emotion

Pretty much nothing is guaranteed these days to disrupt our tranquillity on a near-constant low level more than our interactions on social media. In real life things happen at human speed but on the internet everything is so fast and furious. Whether it's an opinion that you disagree with, having your own opinion challenged or reading information that makes you angry, passionate, fired up or depressed, the algorithms of social media are engineered to serve up content and takes that are guaranteed to stir a response and attract and maintain our attention.

Content that sparks an intense emotional reaction is likely to go viral, meaning it's more likely to end up in our feeds and more likely to inflame passion and strong emotions. It's hard not to get caught up, particularly when the whole system is designed to attract and hold our attention for as long as possible. The social media giants don't want you putting down your phone and enjoying your day outside with your friends or your kids; they want you on your phone, on the platform—engaged in the unpaid labour of providing content, reactions, engagement and your time.

Unless we want to have an unhealthy and addictive relationship with social media—and carry that unhappiness, tension, division and distraction into our 'real' lives—we need a conscious way of engaging with social media.

These platforms *do* serve some good—connecting people, igniting new ideas and elevating new voices—but, like anything that's addictive and triggers our animal brain, it needs to be treated with caution.

You'd think that a philosophy that was developed thousands of years before social media came on the scene would not be helpful in how to use and navigate social media but Stoicism has several useful tips and tools for being online, wisely.

Make sure you only act on good information

Had there been social media in Ancient Greece or Rome, of course Zeno, Chrysippus, Epictetus, Seneca and all the others would have been using it. In its pure form, social media is a great way of connecting people, creating a community of people replicating the more physical forms on the steps of the painted porch (the Stoa, that Stoicism takes its name from) in Athens, or a web of connections and conversations that would have existed between the philosophy schools of the time.

Imagine Zeno arriving after the shipwreck, his cargo of purple dye ruined—stuck in a strange place. He has some time on his hands and wants to learn philosophy, so he might send out a tweet: 'Hi—stuck in Athens for a bit and looking for any recs for a good philosopher—not too expensive!!! Pls Retweet!!' This is social media operating well, where we can seek and find useful, reliable information that will help us to improve our character.

The dangers of misinformation

But Stoics were careful about the information they acted on. They prized rational thinking, acting on solid information and contemplating the situation fully rather than behaving rashly or from a place of panic and anxiety. Social media can be a bin-fire of misinformation, opinion, fear-mongering and virtue signalling, all of which obscures plain information and facts.

You can't judge something rationally if you have bad information. The first thing to ask when you are consuming information on social media is does this give me good information or is it misinformation? If it's misinformation or not from a recognised source, disregard it.

Epictetus could have been talking about social media when he said:

Most of what passes for legitimate entertainment is inferior or foolish and only caters to or exploits people's weaknesses. Avoid being one of the mob who indulges in such pastimes. Your life is too short and you have important things to do. Be discriminating about what images and ideas you permit into your mind. If you yourself don't choose what thoughts and images you expose yourself to, someone else will, and their motives may not be the highest. It is the easiest thing in the world to slide imperceptibly into vulgarity. But there's no need for that to happen if you determine not to waste your time and attention on mindless pap.

YOU DON'T NEED TO HAVE AN OPINION ON EVERYTHING

Ask yourself: why do you need to weigh in on every issue going? Why do you need to proffer your thoughts on nuclear power, Covid vaccines, the unemployment rate, immigration policy, *The Bachelorette*, the new cast of *Survivor*, bitcoin, the latest missing-person story? Surely you are not an expert on all these things? Why does the world need to hear from you about everything? (Or as US comedian Bo Burnham asks in *Inside*: 'Here's a question for you guys. Um . . . Is it . . . is it necessary? Is it necessary that every single person on this planet, um, expresses every single opinion that they have on every single thing that occurs all at the same time? Is that . . . is that necessary? Um . . . Or to ask in a slightly different way, um, can . . . can anyone shut the fuck up?')

There is another way.

You can't control, for example, the nuclear capabilities of France, but so many people tweet about things such as these as if they can control them. These things are not asking to be judged by you. Leave them alone.

If any Stoic advice would make today's world a better place it is that, as Marcus Aurelius said: 'You always own the option of having no opinion.' In these divisive times, how many fights have been had between friends, colleagues or family that could have been avoided had people just kept their opinions to themselves?

Outrage is contagious

Have you ever opened the internet, maybe first thing in the morning, with a calm, clear mind and quickly been drawn into the latest outrage of the day? Maybe it's someone who expressed the wrong opinion and they are being cancelled or publicly shamed, or maybe it's an injustice that happened somewhere in the world that a lot of people are tweeting about. Whatever it is, social media algorithms can create a feedback loop that amplifies outrage and, before you know it, you also are calling for someone to be cancelled or are outraged on behalf of the citizens of some faraway country.

Seneca could have been talking about modern social media pile-ons and cancel culture when he wrote this in *Moral Letters to Lucilius*:

> To consort with the crowd is harmful; there is no person who does not make some vice attractive to us, or stamp it upon us, or taint us unconsciously therewith. Certainly, the greater the mob with which we mingle, the greater the danger.
>
> Withdraw into yourself, as far as you can. Associate with those who will make a better man of you. Welcome those whom you yourself can improve. The process is mutual; for men learn while they teach. Your good qualities should face inwards.

If you do use social media, the Stoics would advise to be restrained and not brag too much or use it as a platform to endlessly self-promote. 'In public, avoid talking often and excessively about your accomplishments and dangers, for however much you enjoy recounting your dangers, it's not so pleasant for others to hear about your affairs,' said Epictetus.

The Stoic virtue of moderation will serve you well when engaging with social media.

You don't need to be right

A lot of the heat and energy on social media is people operating in a binary: 'I am right and you are wrong.' How much energy is spent trying to win an argument, own someone, or cling onto a much-cherished position that may no longer serve you?

If we got rid of our need to be right all the time, then social media might be a place that it was for a brief time in the mid-2000s—a place of wit, jokes, fun, sharing news stories, hot takes, book and music recommendations and on-the-ground information about unfolding news. Now it's a partisan swamp because we have separated into tribes that are using these platforms to fight ideological battles to the death.

Wisdom—one of the four Stoic virtues—comes from being able to absorb and interact with points of view different from your own. It also comes from evolving and learning all the time.

'If someone is able to show me that what I think or do is not right, I will happily change,' Marcus Aurelius said, who sounds like he would have been great on Old Twitter. 'For I seek the truth, by which no one ever was truly harmed. Harmed is the person who continues in his self-deception and ignorance.'

Dealing with insults

Whether you receive an insult or shade via social media or it happens at work or a party, the result is likely to be the same: your tranquillity will be disturbed. The insult is a rock being thrown into the calm pool of our mind, and its effects ripple out and can create ongoing tension and disturbances.

Insults can provoke our anger, our desire for revenge, our lust for getting back at the other person and returning fire, or the need to be right. These are all things that damage character, so, as usual, the Stoics thought a lot about how to cope with insults so that they could carry on with life without the extra stress.

The Stoic response to insults is both clever and hilarious. And centuries down the road, their techniques still work when it comes to being insulted on social media or in real life.

Is the insult true?

It was a public holiday, there was free public transport and the city was jammed. I was racing from Circular Quay station to the Manly ferry terminal, with four minutes to get down two flights of stairs, through a thick, slow-moving crowd. Stress kicked in—I could not miss this ferry, and miss this lunch. So, using sharp elbows, I barged through the crowd, hitting a woman passer-by harder than I intended in the ribs. I am not proud of this. It was a poor reflection on my character that I would be prepared to physically harm a stranger in order to get to lunch on time. The woman let loose a string of expletives about me as I pushed past her, including the fact that I was rude and aggressive.

The first Stoic strategy when being insulted is to pause and ask yourself: is this insult true?

In this case, the insult was true. I was rude and aggressive. The insult therefore wasn't upsetting. But what upset me for much of the day was that I had been rude and aggressive in the first place, and that my character was damaged by my behaviour. I did not worry about the insult.

How well-informed was the insulter?

Epictetus said, when insulted, to pause and consider how well-informed the insult is. Is it based on misinformation or ignorance? Or is it true?

If it's misinformed, we can ignore the insult or set the insulter right.

Corrections

If I am writing a story and I get a fact wrong, and someone tells me I am wrong (this happens to journalists all the time)—and maybe they tell me harshly in a way that's triggering—such as 'you're stupid, you got the unemployment rate wrong'—then you can accept the correction and see it as helpful. Just ignore the value judgement placed at the start of the correction and be grateful that someone has drawn attention to a mistake that you made that you can then correct. Don't let your ego get involved by needing to be right all the time. 'Reject the sense of injury and the injury itself goes away,' said Marcus Aurelius.

Feeling sorry for the insulter

Recently my house was infested by mice. There was a plague on and the mice in my area had eaten through the bait in record time and they had still not died. I could hear them scratching in the walls at night, and once, one ran out of my shoe, just before I went to put it on. Gross!

I tweeted about this, and received a response from an angry stranger who was living further north where there had been floods and many people had been made homeless.

She tweeted at me, 'Honestly this is so fucking tone deaf. At least you have a house to be infested by mice.'

Once I got over the shock at receiving such a weird and aggressive reply, I waited, and decided not to respond. 'The best answer to anger is silence,' said Marcus Aurelius. He also said childish insults should be the cause for pity rather than anger.

Use humour

The ancient Stoics were famous for using humour to deflect insults.

Cato was pleading a case when an enemy spat in his face. Rather than getting angry, Cato calmly wiped the spit and said, 'I will swear to anyone that people are wrong when they say you cannot use your mouth.' Lol Cato.

Epictetus approved the use of self-deprecating humour. He advised disarming the insulter by saying things like 'if you knew me really well you wouldn't have picked that flaw, I'm actually much worse than you think I am. Perhaps you are an incompetent insulter.'

KEEPING YOUR COOL

When Cato was struck at a bath house, rather than getting angry at the man or punishing him he simply replied when asked about it, 'I don't remember being struck.'

By just blanking the insulter, we have robbed them of the power of seeing us upset. If we just carry on as usual, they will be disconcerted and thrown off balance.

Shield yourself from both flattery and criticism

Part of keeping your tranquillity online is to not fish for praise or engage with trolls or haters.

When I first started writing my Diary for *The Guardian* some of the comments I received were nasty. Now, mostly my articles appear without the ability for people to comment, so I don't get a lot of the early negative feedback that really poisoned my beliefs in myself and my work. But I have to balance this out: that is, if I wasn't seeing the negative feedback, I also had to shield myself from positive feedback and flattery. To receive one without the other was a form of distorted feedback and would give me an unbalanced opinion of myself.

(Feedback from my editors is different. It's their job to either criticise or praise my work—and help me craft it in the best way possible. Criticism can provide valuable information and is a key component of growth—but trolling should not be confused with constructive criticism.)

My decision to engage with outside praise or criticism as little as possible has brought me a delicious freedom to create, not with the mob in mind but my own inner compass. The creation comes from a place of feeling free.

You don't need to be a writer or have work out there in public to take a valuable lesson from this. Being indifferent to the opinions of others (particularly others who do not know us) means you are able to be true to your own nature—a key aspect of Stoicism. And, just as we shouldn't engage with flattery or criticism that comes our way, neither should we dish it out.

The problem with flattery

The Stoics recognised a dark side to flattery: it often hid a truth and disguised an ulterior motive. 'Though shalt not blame or flatter any,' counselled Epictetus. If we are heaped with flattery, we are less likely to try to improve or better ourselves.

Seneca in *Moral Letters to Lucilius* wrote of flattery:

The chief obstacle is that we are quick to be satisfied with ourselves. If we find someone to call us good people, cautious and principled, we acknowledge him. We are not content with a moderate eulogy, but accept as our due whatever flattery has shamelessly heaped upon us. We agree with those who call us best and wisest, although we know they often utter many falsehoods; we indulge ourselves so greatly that we want to be praised for a virtue which is the opposite of our behaviour. A man hears himself called 'most merciful' while he is inflicting torture, 'most generous' while he is plundering, and 'most abstinent' in the midst of drunkenness and lust. So it follows that we don't want to change because we believe we are already excellent.

Stoics would argue that other people's opinion of us is really none of our business. 'Someone despises me—that's their problem,' wrote Marcus. And since their opinion of us is out of our control, there's no point worrying about it anyway. All that matters is how we treat others, our character and acting in accordance with our nature.

Indifference to others' opinions

With social media, we now essentially have two selves that we are shepherding through the world. In the last 15 years, we have doubled the workload of what it is to be human. There is our real, actual self that exists in the physical world, and there's the self that exists online. In addition to the work of our real lives, the work of our online selves is relentless. Creating, defending, promoting and protecting our avatars is exhausting work that is not numerated and is never-ending.

It's made even more fraught by the suspension of norms that govern face-to-face conduct. We are much more likely to encounter abuse, racism, sexism, judgements and anger online than out in the streets, yet we are not taught how to navigate this world or be resilient in the face of a digital onslaught. It is all too new. As well as the pile-ons, part of the anxiety of being online is the performative aspect—the pressure to be funny, cool, right-on, clever and hot. You are only as successful as your last post. You're only as hot as the number of Likes you get. But the more you practise Stoicism, the more indifferent you become to other people's opinion of you. Seeking approval of others is no longer a goal, because you will know that you can't control others' opinions of you and that tying your self-worth and happiness to someone else's view of you will be unsettling and unstable.

Be happy with what you've got

'He is a wise man who does not grieve for the things which he has not, but rejoices for those which he has.' —Epictetus

'Do not indulge in dreams of having what you have not, but reckon up the chief of the blessings you do possess, and then thankfully remember how you would crave for them if they were not yours.'

—Marcus Aurelius

In June 2021 I lucked upon a beautiful apartment. It was small, only two-and-a-half rooms but it was on Sydney Harbour, with a window in the living room that looked out onto the water. At night I could hear the seabirds and the water lapping at the garden's edge. I had access to a private harbour pool and would lie in the grass on a hot day and cool off by jumping off the diving board.

My little apartment was a haven. I was blissfully happy . . . for a while. Gradually I got to know my neighbours; one day, one of them, Paul, invited me into *his* apartment. Located at the front of the building, Paul's view was so much better than mine. While I got a slice of the harbour, he had the whole pie. I had a bit of a harbour view but, as I was at the back of the building, my window was further away and most of my view was of a brown brick wall. When I returned to my bolthole, it was with a little less joy than when I had departed. Yes I still had a *partial* view, but I was loving my home a little less after comparing my place to my neighbour's.

Then another neighbour, Lisa, invited me into her apartment—and it was even more palatial than Paul's. It boasted views right across Sydney Harbour and was double the size. My apartment in comparison was like a butler's pantry.

Once more, I began to love my little home a little less. This was one thing I had to cut off at the pass. To suddenly be dissatisfied with something that had once filled me with joy was a sign not of the object changing, but of *me* changing. I was entering into a cycle of what psychologists call hedonic adaptation, where my happiness with my current small apartment dissipated and all I wanted was the bigger apartment. And I would not be satisfied until I got it.

The art of being happy with what you've got is one of the biggest lessons in Stoic philosophy—and also in life.

Epictetus famously said wealth consists not in having great possessions, but in having few wants. And that 'the essence of philosophy is that a man should live so that his happiness depends as little as possible from external causes'. This is as anti-capitalist as it comes.

Remember the idea we've discussed in Part 1? Tranquillity comes from being able to control your happiness—that is, not picking something that will make you happy that is essentially out of your control.

Desiring and obtaining a harbour-side apartment with a better view was partially within my control. But think about what would have to happen to get it. One would need to become available (there were only a handful in my building and none of the residents seemed keen to give theirs up) and then I would have to be able to afford it. A quick check online of the prices revealed that the residents of the better apartments were paying a lot more than I was paying. They were paying so much for the privilege of the view that on my current salary, even if an apartment became available, I would be unable to afford it. So I would have to leave a job I really loved and which made me very happy and get another, better paying job. This was not out of the realm of possibility—but this step was truly out of my control. A job would have to come up and a panel of interviewers would have to decide to give me the job. And then there was the risk. In taking a job for money, not happiness, I risked the tranquillity that came with working for a company that I felt aligned with and where I had a strong community of friends and colleagues.

It was a lot of risk and effort for essentially an extra 60 centimetres of window space overlooking the water. Wouldn't it have been better just to keep enjoying the place I had, which was a price I could afford without financial stress and strain (which in turn would also disrupt my tranquillity)?

The Stoics recognised the havoc that hedonic adaptation could wreck on our tranquillity and developed techniques to stop these insatiable desires for more, more, more from unnecessarily running our lives and making life more stressful for us. In their wisdom, they knew that often what we desired could actually ruin our life in ways that we don't consider: that in trying to get more, we have to work more (do you want to spend all your life working?) or, motivated by greed, we are more tempted into crime or corruption. Think of all the white-collar financial crimes committed all because the perpetrators wanted better holidays or a more expensive watch or a more prestigious car. Sydney white-collar criminal Melissa Caddick convinced her elderly parents to mortgage their home so she could invest their money. Instead, she bought a diamond. The lust for things ruined her family, her friends who invested with her, and ultimately herself—she is missing, presumed dead. Like the thief who took Epictetus's lamp, the desire for more or better possessions can be ruinous to character.

But first—what is hedonic adaptation?

Hedonic adaptation, or the hedonic treadmill, happens when the joy and initial rush of new things have faded and we want even more and better things to get to the same point of happiness. This adaptation process is normal and common; when the novelty has worn off a once-desired thing, we become adapted to it, and we incorporate that new thing into the normal landscape of our lives. There are sound, evolutionary reasons that we are programmed to desire new things: it's not a design flaw. If our emotional reactions did not decrease over time, we would not be able to differentiate more significant stimuli (new and important events) from less significant stimuli (old events that should fade into the background). Without being able to become used to new stimuli, we would become overwhelmed with emotion and unable to change or survive.

But we have definitely turned the dial up too high on hedonic adaptation: fast fashion that is worn once or twice then ends up as landfill; cheap furniture and homewares from Ikea or Kmart that are not built to last but must be replaced each year; the latest technology that is quickly superseded as an incentive for consumers to

216

buy more products that they do not need. We have abundance but everything is kind of shitty and degraded.

Paul Theroux wrote the novel *The Mosquito Coast* in the 1980s, but the consumerism his character despises in this passage has since gone up several levels into hyper-drive: 'We eat when we're not hungry, drink when we're not thirsty, buy what we don't need, and throw away everything that's useful. Don't sell a man what he wants—sell him what he doesn't want. Pretend he's got eight feet and two stomachs and money to burn. That's not illogical—it's evil.'

And also terribly sad. The beautiful and sensitive surface of the earth, our magnificent and complex oceans are now where all the cheap plastic crap that we use so briefly goes to rest . . . forever.

This destruction of our only planet has resulted in part from hedonic adaptation, the very same destructive force that also creates such an immense internal disturbance that we will spend the best years of our lives working so we can afford more and newer *things*. We don't seem to realise (or more depressingly, we *do* realise) that the things we waste our life accumulating are actually going to exacerbate issues for the planet, and that the next generation is going to be left to clean up.

'There's always more to do'

Philosophers understood how the hedonic treadmill could leave us in a frequent state of dissatisfaction as pleasure in new goods, people and experiences eventually wore off over time. Epicurus, who founded the Epicurean school of philosophy in Ancient Greece around the same time as Stoicism, gave this matter a lot of thought.

He believed that there were some core desires like the need for food, drink and shelter. But we could also be hostage to empty desires, such as the need for fame or success. These goals never feel fulfilled as there always seems to be more to do, or other people seem more successful than us, and so we never seem to achieve anything. We can slow down this hedonic treadmill by recognising when something is an empty desire and take steps to stop chasing it.

You could argue that people in Ancient times probably found it easier to resist the hedonic treadmill because they were not subject to the barrage of advertising and media that we face today, with not just billboards and ads in newspapers and on television but with screens everywhere, in our pockets and accompanying us into our workdays that also bring targeted advertising into spheres previously untouched by commerce. It can be extremely difficult at this present moment in history to even know we are being advertised to, let alone be able to resist the advertising. But, if we now take a Stoic point of view, like a lot of things in Stoicism, consciousness is key; if we are aware of the hedonic response, and are able to check our desires as they arise, we are some way advanced to taking our power back.

Despite not facing the onslaught of advertising and consumer products, the Greco-Roman age still had prestige goods and items that were highly prized. People used to make ridiculous purchases—say of decorative urns or wines or marble tables—and want to show them off to friends. Alain de Botton, in *The Consolations of Philosophy*, noted how Seneca was particularly fond of cedar tables with marble legs and was said to order 500 of them for a banquet.

But, like most humans, no sooner had Romans got the goods they so desperately once desired, they tired of them and wanted something more. In *Moral Letters to Lucilius*, Seneca warned, 'At last, then, away with all these treacherous goods! They look better to those who hope for them than to those who have attained them.'

His meaning was the joy is in the anticipation of goods (or as you probably have experienced, in the anticipation of a holiday or a parcel arriving from Amazon) than in the actual experience of ownership itself.

Of particular one-upmanship in Roman times among the wealthy elites were ultra-competitive banquets. As well as serving game meats, seafood and spices from across the Roman empire, hosts competed by serving over-the-top, exotic dishes like stuffed dormouse and parrot-tongue stew. Huge numbers of parrots were raised and slaughtered for the dish. Banquets went for hours and involved multiple courses plus wine. Men ate lying down, the better to digest their meals. People went into debt to pay for these culinary orgies. One famous epicurean, Apicius, allegedly killed himself because he had gone broke after throwing too many lavish banquets.

Marcus Aurelius, for whom money was no object, tried to temper any lust for material things—including extravagant banquets—by reminding himself what they really were. As we saw in the chapter 'How to be Moderate', he reframed the food and drink before him as dead bodies and the juice of mouldy grapes.

I did this exercise too, and reminded myself that I would have to upend my life and work day and night for money to get 60 centimetres more window and a slightly larger room to shower in. I reminded myself that I could have an unlimited view of the water—for free—if only I were to go outside.

Coming from an age of riches, decadence and hedonism not unlike our own, the ancients understood the hedonic treadmill well and the need to protect yourself against its forces (or at least be conscious of them).

They devised a few strategies to assist.

Preferred indifferents

As you will be aware from the chapter on 'How to Cope with Disaster', we never know when we'll have a change in circumstances, or what will result in a loss. So Stoics tried to prepare for unexpected losses through the doctrine of preferred indifferents.

A reason for resisting the hedonic treadmill—and the lure of new objects, goods, people and experiences—is that many of these things are outside our control. As we have explored, these things—including wealth, assets, property and non-tangibles such as praise, a good relationship, fame and a good reputation—are out of our control and therefore they should be seen as a preferred indifferent.

It's more important to keep your tranquillity than spend all your hours scheming how to get more money so you can buy a more elevated property, or a house with a better view, or a prestige car.

You can ruin your present by mortgaging for a future material good that you may never purchase. And even if you do spend all your hours working to get the Lexus, a Stoic would say you might die on your way to the showroom, so you wasted the bit of life and freedom you had by living in the future and not appreciating what you already have. As we saw in the chapter 'How to be Mortal', time is the only currency that is really valuable and irreplaceable.

As Seneca put it:

Putting things off is the biggest waste of life: it snatches away each day as it comes, and denies us the present by promising the future. The greatest obstacle to living is expectancy, which hangs upon tomorrow, and loses today. You are arranging what lies in Fortune's control, and abandoning what lies in yours. What are you looking at? To what goal are you straining? The whole future lies in uncertainty: live immediately.

Negative visualisation

In order to break the cycle of hedonic adaptation, the Stoics undertook negative visualisation.

The goal of negative visualisation is not to scare us when thinking that we could lose these things that we had once so desired and lusted after, but rather it's to drum into us that all we have is 'on loan' and that anything we have could be lost to us at any time. So a great apartment, a good-looking partner, a prestigious and interesting job, a rare piece of jewellery—all this isn't ours forever. In the case of hedonic adaptation when it comes to partners—so-called trading up is particularly fraught as you are vulnerable to the other person leaving *you* for someone better, and riding their own hedonic treadmill.

By imagining losing something or someone, it's a way for us to appreciate and savour the things we currently have. We may not have these things forever (after all, they are on loan), and so we need to appreciate them while we have them in our custody.

Seneca wrote: 'Remember that all we have is "on loan" from Fortune, which can reclaim it without our permission, indeed, without even advance notice.'

It could always be worse—an exercise in negative thoughts

In relation to my conundrum of loving my apartment less after seeing my neighbours' apartments, the exercise of negative visualisation goes something like this. Instead of coveting my neighbour Paul's view from his apartment, imagine having no view at all. Imagine your apartment is on the sub-basement level, with bars on the windows overlooking a dark and smelly laneway where the bins are kept.

Since I've lived in an apartment (or several) that fits this description, it is not too hard to imagine. There was one in particular in Potts Point. I had a happy year there but the apartment was half in a basement and had bars on the window. I remember waking up to a gloom and just the tiniest shard of light filtering through the windows and not being able to open this window on hot days because of the stench of the bins. I sit down and remember all of this then open my eyes. And where am I? I am in the apartment where I currently live—with a beautiful window that looks down on a large, blue square of water—and lets in a good amount of light. I open the window and smell the briny scent of the harbour and hear the tinkle of the boats bobbing. And then I am filled with gratitude for where I live and am thankful to have this abundance when previously I just had darkness and rubbish bins.

If I had still been in that old, gloomy Potts Point apartment and doing this exercise, then I would have negatively visualised another apartment I had lived in. This one was in Manhattan. I wasn't there for very long but it made an impression on me for its sheer unliveability. It was fully in a basement, the size of a cupboard and had no proper window, only a tiny lightwell that led to a grate that opened out on the pavement. I could see people's shoes as they walked past. Sometimes I thought I saw rats. I definitely *heard* rats. There was very little ventilation and it was immediately stressful entering the apartment as it was incredibly claustrophobic.

When I was there and feeling very stressed about being in such a small space that was evidently not designed to be lived in, I negatively visualised the alternative—that is, I lived in Central Park.

Even in a very uncomfortable place, negative visualisation made me grateful I had it.

And had I actually been sleeping in Central Park, negative visualisation would be imagining being sick and sleeping in the park, or being attacked sleeping in the park, or having no pleasant park to sleep in and having to sleep on the sidewalk.

The exercise works like a Russian doll. At each point on the journey you contain within you an idea of a smaller, less pleasant place. You can use negative visualisation to imagine that you are somewhere worse than you presently are. And the feeling that should arise then when you come out of the exercise is gratitude.

You can do the exercise anywhere that is quiet and you can close your eyes and bring the images to mind. I sat in my underappreciated apartment and did it. And here I was—ten or so years later—in a stunning part of the world, an apartment on Sydney Harbour, worth around 1.5 million dollars, and I was still needing to practise the same technique as when I lived in a grim windowless box.

It just shows how insidious hedonic adaptation is and how we have to guard against it.

LET GRATITUDE FLOW

At the root of this practice is gratitude. When the things we have no longer excite us and we long for something new, negative visualisation will show us the truth of the situation: that is, what we have was something that we once desperately desired, and that we should be grateful for.

After all, 'It is not the man who has too little, but the man who craves more, that is poor,' said Seneca.

Avoiding the desire to be famous

Did I want to be famous? No. But I did want to be *known*: I wanted to have a good reputation for my work, and I wanted that reputation to extend beyond the boundaries of my immediate circles. Was being known beyond the people *I knew*, something that was driven by ego? Was it a low-key, regional version of fame? And if so, why did I seek it? What harm lay there? Should the urge be perhaps something to cast off, instead following the Stoic program to only want things that were in my control?

One of the things I had discussed with Andrew over the years, even before our interest in Stoicism kicked off, was the need for recognition—and how this is a driver for human happiness and base satisfaction.

Living in ancient times, or alive now—the thirst for recognition is a constant no matter what the age. It's a way of stamping the words 'I am Here' on the world. The need to be known by others (or in modern parlance—to be *seen*) takes place in concentric circles. There's the need to be known and recognised by an intimate partner, by your family, in your friendship group, at work.

Then broader still is the need to be thought of positively by acquaintances and then a desire to be known and appreciated in the public sphere, among strangers. This last one is 'fame'—and the desire for it was as problematic in Stoic times as it is now in the modern age, where celebrities are worshipped as if they were Greek gods.

While recognition can be a great building block for our self-esteem, and can make us feel valued and important, Stoicism has some strong words for those who seek an amplification of that basic need for recognition, in the form of fame.

'The wise man thinks of fame just enough to avoid being despised,' remarked Epictetus. This is a low bar. What he meant was that you should seek so little of it that as long as you are not hated, that is sufficient. In Alain de Botton's view, the Epicurean school thought so little of fame they labelled the desire for it both unnatural and unnecessary in the list of things needed for happiness. (They also lumped 'power' in with fame, as unnecessary and unnatural, while of the highest order were friends, freedom, thought, food, shelter and clothes.)

Becoming famous is something that lies outside your control, which roused the suspicion of Stoics. Getting fame depends on other people's reactions to your talents, and you cannot control these reactions. As Marcus Aurelius wrote: 'Seek admiration from the people you know. People who seek admiration from those they have never met and never will—they might as well be upset by not being a hero to their great-grandfather.' Ha ha ha—sick burn.

Because fame is at its essence an unstable phenomenon (it comes and goes), the pursuit of it will only disrupt your tranquillity. And this disruption of your tranquillity is too high a price to pay for the fleeting pleasures of fame.

Fame will make you clingy and insecure

Fortunes wax and wane—the only constant in the world is change.

You might attain fame briefly but be unable to really enjoy it due to the anxiety that it may desert you at any moment. Unless you are okay with losing it all overnight, you will never be able to fully relax into it. You risk becoming clingy or insecure trying to hang onto it.

You might gain fame by, say, writing the year's hottest novel, only to be forgotten when the next hyped writer comes along. Or you may get chosen for a reality television show and enjoy recognition for the season that you are on television, only to be forgotten and dropped by the once-clamouring producers and the public, as soon as the next batch of contestants appear the following year. Or you may be CEO of a large company, and courted by the big end of town, only to have the invitations dry up when you retire and no longer have your previous status.

Tying your sense of happiness and wellbeing to fame is like trying to stand up paddleboard on the open seas. The conditions are always changing and you could be thrown off at any moment. Cursing the sea for its waves, currents and tides is useless. Yet we think we can hang onto something as unstable and dynamic as fame. We think we can control the sea and the tides of public opinion.

The Stoics advised that if we try to hang onto the fame, we must give away our power, become people-pleasers and compromise our character. Think of the actors who never evolve, doing sequel after sequel of the same action movie because they want to hang onto the fame of their youth, when they were at the height of their popularity.

As modern Stoic philosopher William Irvine pointed out, 'If we seek social status, we give other people power over us. We have to do things calculated to make them admire us, and we have to refrain from doing things that will trigger disfavour.' This lack of evolving and honouring the inner self can be disastrous for character.

Epictetus went so far to say that the pursuit of fame would only enslave us, as we will be hostage to public opinion and the success of our careers. 'Fame is but the empty noise of madmen,' he said.

We could all name a dozen celebrities, and even a former prime minister or two, who have suffered some misfortune or a bad career move or work choices or a fall from grace or loss of reputation or who simply are burnt out or who have fallen out of fashion, and observed the pain this causes to the previously prominent person. In order to remain in the public eye the famous person must be continually strategising and working, trying to gauge which way the public mood may swing and trying to capture the zeitgeist to retain their once-exalted position. Some celebrities, in a bid to remain relevant and famous, resort to ever more bizarre and attention-seeking behaviours; others try to numb the pain of public indifference through drugs, alcohol or other addictive behaviours. Or else it goes the other way, and the famous person feels trapped by the very thing they once coveted so strongly. All they want to do is disappear. Fame becomes a burden.

The famous then resent their lack of privacy, how a tweet or an Instagram post gets misinterpreted and blows up, or are haunted by the spectre of a lack of trust in their private relationships (how many celebrities, heart sinking, crushed again, have read a story from a 'trusted source' in a tabloid newspaper, selling them out?).

The Stoics in ancient times, well before social media and global celebrity—where word spread at dinners and banquets and in lecture halls—could see, even then—even without the internet!—the problems associated with fame. They were more suspicious of the desire for fame than the desire for money. Money was classified as a 'preferred indifferent' and its presence in your life could be agreeably tolerated (as long as you didn't get too attached). But in fame they saw a more insidious allure. Money could be used to help others, but fame didn't have the same generative quality.

The fundamental element of fame is separation. You are pulled from the pack by virtue of a talent you have or ridiculous luck or suprahuman drive or good looks or an incredible six-pack. But with such profound separation comes not just applause (and the envy you'll attract) but loneliness. Stoics thought we thrived best as social animals, as part of a collective—and fame itself is a very individual experience. By its very nature, it takes us away from the collective.

Don't lust for legacy

Some want fame for the perks it can bring in the here and now; others want fame so they can carve out a legacy.

Chasing posthumous fame or ensuring that we have some sort of legacy for future generations is a folly, according to the Stoics. They didn't see the point in having a statue built in your honour if you were dead and gone. What mattered was what you did while you were alive, your character and whether you made the most of the time you had.

Marcus Aurelius in his usual practical, no-bullshit way, broke the concept of posthumous fame down: 'People who are excited by posthumous fame forget that the people who remember them will soon die too. And those after them in turn. Until their memory, passed from one to another like a candle flame, gutters and goes out.'

Instead, 'Give yourself a gift: the present moment. People out for posthumous fame forget that the generations to come will be the same annoying people they know now. And just as mortal. What does it matter to you if they say x about you, or think y?'

Yes—the annoying people you hated when you were alive will just be replaced by more annoying people who will live on in future generations. So why would you care about impressing these nameless, faceless irritants?

After all, said Marcus Aurelius, once we are dead, it doesn't really matter what happens. 'Alexander the Great and his mule driver both died and the same thing happened to both,' he wrote. That is, we are all food for worms. We are all returned to nature.

Beat FOMO and comparisons

'No person has the power to have everything they want, but it is in their power not to want what they don't have, and to cheerfully put to good use what they do have.' —Seneca

'The object of life is not to be on the side of the majority, but to escape finding oneself in the ranks of the insane.'

—Marcus Aurelius

Whenever I catch up with younger friends, they tell me what they've been up to but also what they've missed out on. Debilitating FOMO—the fear of missing out—is a very millennial trait, but everyone suffers with pangs of it from time to time. No matter where you are, the place where you aren't is more fun.

Social media has given everyone the acute and painful ability to peer out to every social event their friends are enjoying that they haven't been invited to or were not able to attend. It's a panopticon of pain. What a cruel invention and yet somehow we are addicted;

somehow we can't look away. If you were born after 1985, it has always been this way, whereas at least people who grew up in the 1990s were able to go to parties, and not look at their phones and see other better parties going on that they were not invited to. In the past, without phones and social media, they had a better chance of enjoying themselves where they were.

The FOMO is real, and can often end up running their lives. People attend things they don't want to because of FOMO or are eaten up with envy when they see an image of a place or party where they are not. FOMO pulls people out of the enjoyment of the present moment and places them in a state of agitation about what they should or could have been doing. Then there is social exclusion. We are pack animals; we thrive in communities and belonging is tied deeply to wellbeing. Social media and the subsequent FOMO it provokes is in part a response from being excised from the group, not included and perhaps not fitting in. The fear of being left out of the tribe or excluded from the ceremony (or depending on your period of history—excluded from the ball, or from harvest festival or from the concert) is an ancient fear. But we are now in a moveable Hall of Mirrors (thankyou, Instagram) where the fear follows us, and distorts everything.

While I was tempted to place FOMO in the category of Very Modern Problems, the more Stoicism I read, the more I realised that FOMO has always been around, and that the Stoics—of course!—had methods of dealing with it. They eerily predicted and planned for an age where feeling slighted and left out would be a regular occurrence.

The main thing with the Stoic lessons around FOMO is that although some of them may seem a little artificial, they were designed to ensure that we maintain our tranquillity and not get agitated when we feel FOMO coming on.

When you're not invited

The first lesson is a bit of a hard one to pull off . . . It involves being the bigger person—and generous with others.

Summing up the essence of FOMO, Epictetus asked, 'Is anyone preferred before you at an entertainment, or in a compliment, or in being admitted to a consultation?' To translate: is someone at the party you're not at, or been praised or socialised with some VIPs?

Epictetus advised: 'If these things are good, you ought to be glad that he has gotten them; and if they are evil, don't be grieved that you have not got them.'

Essentially, if someone has been invited to a party, and you haven't, you should be glad for them. That's a sign of good character that you can be pleased for others, even while missing out yourself.

The second part of this is: if the things you want but have been excluded from are not good for you (another bottle of wine, the admission into the bathroom stall to partake in a line of cocaine) then you should be glad that you are missing out. This is because the thing you are missing out on could harm your character—the big no-no for the Stoics.

The trade-off

When it comes to FOMO, the Stoics also raised the spectre of the trade-off. One of your friends may have gone to the music festival, and you have FOMO looking at their pictures on social media—but look at what you have: an extra 200 dollars in your pocket by not buying a ticket, the chance to have a good night's sleep and the next morning without a hangover.

When talking of trade-offs, Epictetus (in this translation) used the example of lettuce—but just substitute 'lettuce' for something more fun: a party, a holiday, a festival, a concert . . . 'For how much is lettuce sold? Fifty cents, for instance. If another, then, paying fifty cents, takes the lettuce, and you, not paying it, go without them, don't imagine that he has gained any advantage over you. For as he has the lettuce, so you have the fifty cents which you did not give.'

By missing out on an event, you didn't compromise your integrity by having to suck up to the host or flatter her—and therefore diminish your character or create a social obligation. Epictetus wrote:

> So, in the present case, you have not been invited to such a person's entertainment, because you have not paid him the price for which a supper is sold. It is sold for praise; it is sold for attendance. Give him then the value, if it is for your advantage. But if you would, at the same time, not pay the one and yet receive the other, you are insatiable, and a blockhead. Have you nothing, then, instead of the supper? Yes, indeed, you have: the not praising him, whom you don't like to praise; the not bearing with his behaviour at coming in.

Essayist Adam Phillips, one of the top thinkers in the field of psychoanalysis, in the *London Review of Books* captured the Stoic mindset when he was writing about FOMO:

> Exclusion may involve the awakening of other opportunities that inclusion would make unthinkable. If I'm not invited to the party, I may have to reconsider what else I want: the risk of being invited

233

to the party does my wanting for me, that I might delegate my desire to other people's invitations. Already knowing or thinking we know, what we want is how we manage our fear of freedom. Wanting not to be left out may tell us very little about what we want, while telling us a lot about how we evade our wanting.

So, in short, when you feel a pang of FOMO, remember this advice from the Ancients. Firstly, by not going to the event you are possibly missing out on things that will compromise your character, such as getting too drunk at the party and making a dick of yourself. Secondly, by missing out on one thing, you gain the time and space to occupy yourself with another thing (or at least save some money); and, thirdly, by not attending an event, you avoid having to suck up to or hang out with people you mightn't like very much.

Avoid making comparisons

Closely related to FOMO is the horror of comparisons. Comparing yourself to others is a sure road to unhappiness.

Think about when you were at school, then university. At school everyone was in the same boat, wore the same uniforms, did the same classes together each day and had roughly the same sorts of lives. You might peel away from each other and go to university—but at university, you have a similar experience to your peers. The trouble starts when you graduate. Some may travel or go work in a bar for a few years, while others take high-paying corporate jobs, while others marry young and have families. Suddenly you are not on the same track as your friends. Maybe you feel like you've taken a wrong turn in life. You might feel like you've made dud choices. You get FOMO.

You begin making comparisons and it's not healthy. It may not only damage friendships but it could ruin the enjoyment you might have been having in your own life. By deciding not to compare yourself to others, you will save yourself a lot of pain over the course of your life. This is pain you probably don't even know you were generating because you were making comparisons unconsciously. But if you drop the comparisons, not only will you feel better about your own life, other people will feel better about being around you.

Comparing up and down

Making comparisons can go in two directions, neither of them good. If you compare yourself—say, your job—to a friend who might have a better paying job than you, you are going to feel worse about yourself and your job. But if you compare yourself favourably to someone—for example, a friend who recently lost their job—you are making yourself feel better on the back of someone else's situation. This creates a separation and a division where previously there was none and means you don't see yourself as equal with your friend, but superior (and no one wants to be friends with someone who feels superior to them).

Feeling a twinge of satisfaction when something goes wrong for a friend is not an uncommon feeling. After all, Gore Vidal famously said: 'Every time a friend succeeds, I die a little.' That may be because you are unconsciously in competition with your friend and believe that life is a zero–sum game. When your friend has a loss, you unconsciously feel that you are spared from loss, or that you are not as unlucky as your friend. These thoughts are not rational—but they are common.

The opposite of separation is connection. But we disconnect when we make comparisons. A true friend would never feel satisfaction at a friend's loss. Instead, a true friend would be happy for a friend's successes and sad at their losses.

Part of this schadenfreude we may feel is not our fault. It's just the unconscious way we've been programmed to be pitted against one another.

We are in the waning days of neo-liberalism, it is to be hoped, where such comparisons (and the separation from each other that followed) were encouraged and even seen as natural. We absorbed the dominant scarcity mentality, where unconsciously we see the spoils of the world—whether it be good looks, athleticism, talent, status or money—as finite. Life and resources become a zero–sum game: we can't all share in the good stuff and, if someone wins, then someone must lose. But this is not true! We can all win, particularly if like the Stoics, we measure 'winning' as succeeding at things that are solely within our control such as our character, how we treat others and how we respond to things.

Back to the control test

There are even more reasons to make a conscious effort to stop comparing yourself to others. And that brings us back to the control test.

A Stoic would reject even attempting to make comparisons because trying to get what someone else has is largely out of your control.

Remember: you can only control your own character, how you treat others and how you respond—all else is out of your control, including status, or what others think of you.

Part of making comparisons is tied up with desire—which can so often lead to unhappiness—because the object of your desire is outside your control. Think about all the times you have been in unrequited love. The pain of that is, in large part, having an over-whelming and strong desire to be in a relationship with someone. But we have no control over whether that person loves us in return.

If you desire to have a better character or take better charge of your reactions or actions or treat others better, you will succeed—but anything else and you risk being disappointed because there are factors outside your control at play.

Say you want to earn as much money as your co-worker, as by comparison you are being underpaid. You can try to get promoted or change jobs, but these things aren't entirely up to you, so you are therefore liable to have your tranquillity destroyed by trying to achieve something that is outside your power. You can't control how good someone is at something else, and there will always be people who are better than you at some things, and people who are worse. It would be great if you could give up the comparison game and instead focus on your own race.

You can celebrate other people. Your ego is the enemy in this, but it can be tamed and brought under control. We need to be able to find joy in the success of other people. If we can let go, negativity loses its hold on us, and we are free to live the life we want.

Our goal is to define success for ourselves: that is the only thing that we can control. We cannot control others.

WHEN LIFE GETS TOUGH

The 'no comparisons' rule comes in handy not just for the usual life things—making comparisons about who has the better car or job or the most well-behaved children—but for when life gets suddenly really bleak.

If you are constantly comparing yourself to others in the good times, you're going to really struggle when things go bad.

If you get cancer and require a long period of time receiving brutal treatment or undergoing an arduous recovery, it would be torture to keep comparing yourself to others who might be enjoying their health or just going about their life. In these circumstances, you would be rendered absolutely miserable as you have a double serve of suffering: once from the actual disease and twice from the comparisons where, in your head, you are coming off worse off than others. You do not have control over the disease itself—your body is one of the things that is only in your partial control—but you do have control as to whether you make yourself miserable by constantly comparing yourself to others.

Role models

Of course, in saying 'don't make comparisons', I'm advising you to swim against a very established and strong tide, one that you've probably been swimming with all your life. We all compare ourselves to others and do it without thinking. 'Who am I?' is often discovered and known by reference to our peers and broader society.

Comparisons can result in psychological torment in the form of envy, jealousy and either a superiority or inferiority complex. But there is a Stoic fix for this, allowing us to 'calibrate ourselves against our peers' but without the toxic load of making comparisons. That is to have a role model.

Having a role model fulfils the evolutionary need to have someone in our sights that can provide a baseline measure for what we want to be and what we can achieve. These people don't need to be

Stoics—they can be someone you know, or someone you don't—but whose work, philosophy or life you admire. They don't even have to be alive. Marcus Aurelius—although long dead—has been cited as a role model for people as diverse as Bill Clinton and Zadie Smith.

My own role models are a mixture of people who have achieved a lot professionally in my field and those who live a life that is kind, generous and authentic.

I compare myself to them but strive to make the comparison a positive one, where I don't beat myself up for not achieving their heights but instead use their success to inspire me to do better.

In journalism now, I have seen competitors come and go. Although my career has endured, it has had ups and downs, and there have been plenty of times when colleagues who were my peers raced ahead of me in career progression, earned oodles more money and enjoyed higher profiles. Rather than being eaten up with envy, I've found it better to support people's success. The industry is small, and it's better not to harbour any ill will towards colleagues. You will have far more longevity if you support each other rather than see everyone around you as a threat. The scarcity mindset is a false one, and it will only limit you.

Instead, the colleagues who have done well and whom I admire, I treat as role models. If they do well, it spurs me on and inspires me; if I am feeling stuck in my own work, I can search my role model's name on the internet and read their work and feel revved up when I go back to my own story. I become less stuck.

Seneca gave advice on how to choose a Stoic role model:

Choose someone whose way of life as well as words, and whose very face as mirroring the character that lies behind it, have won your approval. Be always pointing him out to yourself either as your guardian or as your model. There is a need, in my view, for someone as a standard against which our characters can measure themselves. Without a ruler to do it against you won't make crooked straight.

How to use comparisons

The best comparison is the one that you make with yourself. Are you doing better now than you did a year ago? Are you coping better? You just need to be better than yourself, or doing the best that you can do.

The Stoics kept a diary as a vehicle for contemplation and a way of measuring self-development. When you keep a diary, you can look back and assess whether you have changed or made progress from a year ago, or two years ago or ten years. A diary will give you a clean picture of what you were going through back then. The only comparison you should make is with your past self.

Diaries are a great cathartic space for you to pour out feelings that may be too raw and ugly for public consumption. You may not believe it at the time, but feelings do fade. To read back over your past self in the grip of big pain is unpleasant. But we forget the texture and minute details of deep emotional and physical pain for a reason. To have a permanent ongoing memory of the depths of your despair would be to remind yourself of why you should never love or trust again. So nature gave us forgetting. Ideally, a diary gives you a little taste of your old pain, without triggering the feelings we had at the time we went through difficulties.

Looking back also places past pain in context. Looking back, now for me it's clear any success I enjoy now was built on the fruits of failed labour: the unpublished novels, a sixteen-part TV series set in a newsroom that never got made, plays that were written but never performed. It's okay. It doesn't really matter that those things never took off. They were part of the apprenticeship I realised I had been doing only once it was completed.

Beat anxiety

'Man is not worried by real problems so much as by his imagined anxieties about real problems.'   —**Epictetus**

'Wild animals run from the dangers they actually see, and once they have escaped them worry no more. We however are tormented alike by what is past and what is to come. A number of our blessings do us harm, for memory brings back the agony of fear while foresight brings it on prematurely. No one confines his unhappiness to the present.'   —**Seneca**

It's the start of 2022, and I'm at the dentist getting fitted for a mouthguard to wear at night to protect the enamel on my teeth, which has been worn down by constant grinding.

I'm vaguely embarrassed by this. I thought I was chill, relaxed, *ataraxic*. I mean, maybe I have been a little anxious. But it's been a time!

I'm not the only one, says the dentist. He's run off his feet fitting mouthguards to the anxious people of Sydney whose bodies are trying to expel anxiety by grinding their teeth at night.

President of the Victorian branch of the Australian Dental Association, Jeremy Sternson, told the ABC that 2021 had been the year of the cracked tooth. 'Normally in a year you may see a handful of these patients, but we were seeing three or four of these a day,' he said. People were coming in with neck, jaw and face pain, or cracked teeth, with dentists blaming stress as the cause.

What can you say about anxiety—except it's pretty much the default state of almost everyone, all the time, right now. There's been no let up for years (when did it start—2018? Or 2014? Or 2020?), and it's the rare person who hasn't experienced 4 a.m. wakings, the seesaw of emotion made manifest in the physiological feeling of dread in the stomach, the racing heart and the premonition of a panic attack at 10 p.m. in the supermarket at the emptied-out toilet paper aisle. It's also the rare person who hasn't been heartsick and afraid, closed down their tabs, and switched off from the news because they couldn't bear One More Thing. Then there are the mind games and pretending— trying to convince yourself at the start of a fresh day, that, if you don't look at the news, all the things happening out there *aren't really happening*, and you can build a New Jerusalem if not in your home then in your head, untouched by the world out there, which really has *nothing to do with you* and your family, because really you are not a big player, you just go to work and want to pay your mortgage and raise your kids—and block the rest out . . . and so you fervently pretend there's no chaos raging outside your door.

So—on we roll. The anxiety accumulates—a build-up on the bones, a hardening of the tender matter around the heart, a speedy cortisol-firing feeling of fast-racing blood through the body, followed by frequent dips into a new, draggier exhaustion that sometimes seems it will never lift. Have you ever been this tired? Has anyone ever been this tired as you are now? No. No. No. It's not possible.

Then there's the darkness visible, the weak, bleak moments—strung together like fairy lights at the party at the end of the world. There is this Doomsday feeling that you swear you've never quite had like this before. In these moments of deep anxiety those who didn't have children feel a sad sort of relief—and those who did, a complicated kind of guilt.

The anxiety from the pandemic has, for me at least, merged into a more amorphous anxiety about the planet.

In the summer of 2022 we were meant to 'get back to normal' but the signs of disorder were everywhere. The rain would not stop. Cows were washing up on beaches in northern New South Wales—which would have been funny if it weren't so dystopian, and the cows themselves didn't look so odd walking, confused, along the sand. In Lismore, people were cutting holes in their roofs to desperately clamber above the rising waters. One woman's house caught fire *while* it was being flooded. In Sydney the rain lasted for months, while Perth baked through its hottest summer yet. Throughout this strange season came the refrain: 'When are we going to go back to having a normal summer?'

Contemplating—and living through—this disordered summer, it was tempting to let terrifying apocalyptic thinking slip in. If we were no longer living in a world that we recognised, that no longer provided the certainties that gave our lives a reassuring rhythm, the effect was to be destabilising. We begin to feel untethered from the earth itself and its psychologically satisfying seasonal rhythms.

But this is not an anxiety unique to our age. Ancient Stoic philosophers believed the earth would be periodically destroyed by fire (Ekpyrosis) in a ritual cleansing before starting again. Stoics usually believed this event occurred when civilisation was at its very height of sophistication and complexity (like ours is now). In an echo of the modern environmental movement, Stoics believed that when the intact and perfect balance of nature called Gaia was interfered with, then collapse was inevitable.

Seneca believed Ekpyrosis would take the form of a flood. In his brilliant play *Thyestes*, the chorus asks: 'Is nature capable of even/ Greater horrors?'

The messenger replies: 'You think no worse is possible?/This is the prelude.'

The ghost of Thyestes says: 'Nature has been subverted/I have worked damnable confusion, so father equals *his* father and both the son/Grandsons turn into sons, and day turns night.'

You think no worse is possible?/This is the prelude. Down nearly two millennia of time, nearly 730,000 days and nights, Seneca's anxiety meets our own.

In another echo—this one of fears of hyper-globalisation in today's world—James Romm, in his excellent biography of Seneca, *Dying Every Day*, wrote of Seneca's unease as Rome expanded beyond its territorial boundaries.

As in the biblical tale of the Tower of Babel, the very complexity of civilisation seemed to carry the seeds of its own destruction . . . Where once a single ship had disturbed the natural order, Rome had now filled the seas with traffic, scrambling the races and dissolving global boundaries. In Seneca's view . . . the ceaseless advance of the empire would turn the cosmos itself into an enemy. When everyone could go everywhere, when no boundary remained intact, total collapse might not be far off.

It can be tempting to just accept anxiety as being a modern affliction that arrived with smart phones and intensified with the pandemic and climate collapse, but the Stoics referred to it regularly in their writing. Their anxiety about the climate was also acute (but, unlike the climate anxiety of our age, was not backed up by science and reams of data).

There is also the anxiety of everyday life, which the Stoics also sought to deal with. This anxiety might be fear of not having enough money, fear of losing a loved one, relationship or position, or it might be fear of getting sick, or fear of dying. It could be the anxiety of a job interview or having a crush, or public speaking. Or it could be more general and free-floating—just the existence of fear itself, a feeling in the body, a dread and the sense of an oncoming panic attack, which has such an extraordinary and powerful capacity to ruin tranquillity.

Never fear! Many of the Stoic teachings are formulated with this anxiety in mind. The Stoics even tried to harness anxiety for good, as a way of testing their virtue.

Developing resilience

The Stoics welcomed hard times, like a well-prepared student welcomes an exam. The Stoics saw their life (and the cultivation of the virtues) as training for moments such as the one we are in now (and they were in, then), where character, resilience, wisdom and courage are tested.

Epictetus said: 'The greater the difficulty, the more glory in surmounting it. Skilful pilots gain their reputation from storms and tempests.'

He saw crisis as a way of unmasking who you really are: 'Circumstances don't make the man, they only reveal him to himself.'

Resilience is a muscle that can be built, rather than something inherited. Using the control test, our character is within our control—and developing resilience is a crucial part of developing character.

Modern Stoic author William Irvine advises to treat setbacks as Stoic tests in order to surmount problems, create resilience and limit negative emotions. One thing he said that we need to surmount when doing this is the subconscious mind, which is always looking to blame and judge when you run into difficulties. These things are antithetical to Stoicism, and so 'by treating a setback as a Stoic test, we take our subconscious mind out of the setback–response loop. More precisely we preclude it from suggesting a finger-pointing explanation for a setback, an explanation that someone else is taking advantage of us or abusing us.'

When this happens, our emotions aren't triggered to the extent they otherwise would have been, which enables our rational thinking mind to step in, and also allows us not to suffer a higher emotional cost of the setback. Irvine said 'the biggest cost by far is the emotional distress a setback triggers'.

If we handle setbacks well, we not only avoid negative emotions but we experience positive emotions, including pride, satisfaction and joy after meeting the challenge, according to Irvine.

When we meet a setback rationally and clearly, taking it on without blaming anyone, and rising to the challenge, we are also exercising courage, one of the four virtues. Courage is crucial in helping build resilience, because it is the engine that powers us through tough situations, and gives us awareness and knowledge that we can do hard things.

Without setbacks, we won't know if we are courageous or not.

Irvine gave the example of a young man called John, who was coddled and protected by his parents from the difficulties of the world. When John becomes an adult, he lacks resilience to cope with setbacks and instead 'experiences a potent mix of hostility and despair. Likewise, instead of regarding the failures he experiences as stepping stones on the road to eventual success, he might regard them simply as traumatic events. John might also be quick to take offence at the things other people say or do, even though they are going out of their way to avoid offending him.'

John is emotionally fragile, and lacks grounding to help stabilise him when hard times come. Irvine contrasts this with John's hypothetical great-grandparents who lived through World War II, facing many setbacks and armed conflict but were 'stronger and more appreciative of life than they had formerly been'.

Irvine posed the interesting question of how can a generation living in peace and prosperity be more emotionally fragile and unhappy than those who have lived through difficult times. The answer, he said, is because they have not been tested and they have not developed resilience.

I think the generation of young people who missed out on two years of education because of Covid and face the pointy end of the climate crisis will be more resilient than their parents. These younger people have had to develop extraordinary resilience and flexibility over the last two years, and have sacrificed a lot so that others much older than them may be safe from the worst effects of Covid. Not enough gratitude has been shown by our leaders for the sacrifices that children have made. I look forward to seeing these courageous young people move into the world after taking on so many of their own Stoic challenges, so young.

In today's world we can seek to rid ourselves of anxiety by going to therapy and addressing the root causes of the anxiety, we can take medication that changes our brain chemistry in an effort to reduce anxiety, we can numb our anxiety with drugs or alcohol or we can avoid anxiety by limiting our exposure to the things that make us anxious.

Different people use different tools, but another element to the tool kit is a range of Stoic exercises and principles to follow that can help lessen or ease anxiety.

Be vigilant about what information you take in

It's hard to be calm if you're doomscrolling hours a day through news websites and social media. The proliferation of fake news has only made doomscrolling more fraught. Is what you are reading true? What information can you trust? And what information should you act on? No wonder we are confused and anxious.

A Stoic would recommend you to be careful of what media and opinions you consume during times of anxiety, such as the pandemic or wars. Counselled Epictetus: 'Other people's views and troubles can be contagious. Don't sabotage yourself by unwittingly adopting negative, unproductive attitudes through your associations with others.'

Stoics prized rational thinking, acting on good information and contemplating the situation fully rather than acting rashly or from a place of panic and anxiety. Marcus Aurelius coped by not allowing his thoughts to be overrun by negativity. 'The universe is change; our life is what our thoughts make of it,' he wrote in his diary.

How this may look for you includes sticking to only one or two trusted news sources and limiting the time you check the news and social media. There is a fine line between being informed and being overwhelmed and swamped with information. Ideally pick a time in the morning and a time in the afternoon or before you have dinner, where you check the news of the day from a reputable source. Live the rest of your hours concerned with your own life and that of the people around you, rather than being carried away, worrying and anxious about the worst things happening to people far away, whose situation you are unable to immediately influence or change.

Using the control test to calm anxiety

'There is only one way to happiness and that is to cease worrying about things which are beyond our power or our will,' said Epictetus.

Once again, initially everything should run through Epictetus's control test. The only things within our control are our character, our actions and responses and how we deal with others. Everything else is out of our control.

Let's say you get a cryptic message from your boss asking you to come in and see her on Monday. It's the sort of message that can unleash the anxiety hounds. Your first reaction might be that you had made a mistake and your boss is going to tear you apart. The anxiety response is fear. But let's interrogate this like a Stoic: if you had not done anything wrong at work, had been of good character, and were performing your duties well, then you have nothing to worry about.

Or maybe you have another anxiety that the meeting is about the company being in trouble and redundancies on the horizon. If this is your anxiety, then examine it. Using the control test, you'll realise that if this is true, then any job losses are out of your control. With this, when something is out of your control then you need to let the anxiety go and let the situation take its course.

The anxious among us will recognise that this is easier said than done, but using our rational mind to confront fears and anxieties is the first step towards rationalising our way out of fear and into the great Stoic virtue of courage. Courage allows you to bear bad news with strength and continue on with a minimum of suffering.

PREFERRED INDIFFERENTS: THE STOLEN LAMP

Whenever we become anxious about losing something—whether it be a person, or goods, or wealth—we should remember that possession of these things is beyond our control, and that, although some of these things are to be *preferred*, we should remain *indifferent* to whether we have them or not.

Epictetus used the example about his stolen lamp (which we covered in the chapter 'How to Be Good'): 'I keep an iron lamp by the side of my household gods, and, on hearing a noise at the window, I ran down. I found that the lamp had been stolen. I reflected that the man who stole it was moved by no unreasonable motive. What then? Tomorrow, I say, you will find one of earthenware. Indeed, a man loses only that which he already has.'

There are a lot of lessons in this passage, but, in regards to anxiety, I use it to reflect on the fact that we should not be anxious about the loss of things, because things—a lamp, a job, money, even friendships—will come and go. The only thing that we should worry about and keep focused on is our own character. And as our character and its development are entirely within our control, then there is no need to be anxious about it.

Put one foot in front of the other

Marcus Aurelius's instructions should be remembered when we are feeling overwhelmed by anxiety. That is, to 'not be overwhelmed by what you imagine, but just do what you can and should'.

Put one foot in front of the other and just focus on the present moment, said the Stoics. This means not being lost in reveries of the past, or fantasies and fears of the future, but just dealing with what is in front of you right now.

'Caretake this moment. Immerse yourself in its particulars. Respond to this person or that person, this challenge, this deed. Quit the evasions. Stop giving yourself needless trouble. It is time to really live; to fully inhabit the situation you happen to be in right now. You are not some disinterested bystander. Participate. Exert yourself,' said Epictetus.

Training for discomfort

Stoics, back in ancient times and today, have a number of practices that involve making themselves deliberately uncomfortable. These include taking ice baths, walking on a hard road in bare feet, fasting, and making themselves open to ridicule by wearing silly clothes in public, as we explored in 'How to Cope with Disaster'. The idea behind this is that, if you endure hardship, discomfort or deprivation, you immunise yourself against future hardship that one day you will be without food, or heating or nice clothes.

Musonius Rufus said that by training himself to be uncomfortable, he was training himself to be courageous. And remember that Seneca, in *Moral Letters to Lucilius*, advised: 'Set aside a certain number of days, during which you shall be content with the scantiest and cheapest fare, with coarse and rough dress, saying to yourself the while: "Is this the condition that I feared?"'

If you successfully fast or live on vastly reduced means, you have robbed fate of the chance to take you by surprise when bad times come. You have already been in training—and know that you can endure a crisis. (*'Is this the condition that I feared?'*)

'If you would not have a man flinch when the crisis comes, train him before it comes,' said Seneca.

The extraordinary case of James Stockdale

There is a teeny-tiny book with a big story that will tell you more about Stoicism in action, than any how-to guide (including this one).

It is a speech given in London in 1993 by Vice Admiral James Stockdale, later published under the title *Courage Under Fire: Testing Epictetus's doctrines in a laboratory of human behavior.*

What you need to know about Stockdale's life before then is that Stockdale 'came to the philosophical life as a 38-year-old naval pilot in grad school at Stanford University'.

It was 1962, and he was in his second year, studying international relations with the aim of becoming a strategic planner at the Pentagon.

Happenstance struck—as it so often does with Stoicism. Taking a break from his regular curriculum, Stockdale 'cruised into Stanford's philosophy corner one winter morning'.

With his grey hair, Stockdale was initially mistaken for a fellow professor by Philip Rhinelander, the Dean of Humanities and Sciences, who taught a philosophy class. The two men hit it off—and to make up for Stockdale's lack of background in philosophy, they arranged to meet for an hour a week for a private tutorial. In the last session, Rhinelander gave Stockdale a copy of Epictetus's *Enchiridion*.

According to Stockdale, Rhinelander explained that Epictetus, the former slave, 'gleaned wisdom rather than bitterness from his early first hand exposure to extreme cruelty and first hand observations of the abuse of power and self-indulgent debauchery' in Ancient Rome. Stockdale took to Epictetus, finding his writing plain-speaking and appealing.

In 1965, back on active duty, Stockdale was in Vietnam in the cockpit of a plane. He was flying low, at treetop level, when he was shot down by Vietcong. After he was ejected and was falling to earth, 'I had about 30 seconds to make my last statement in freedom . . . and so help me, I whispered to myself, "Five years down there, at least. I'm leaving the world of technology and entering the world of Epictetus."'

Once Stockdale hit the ground he was pummelled all over before a man in a police helmet badly broke his leg. Once again, Epictetus was there to help with the preferred indifferents: 'Lameness is an impediment to the Leg, but not to the Will.'

Stockdale was taken to a nearby prison where he spent seven-and-a-half years leading a group of around 50 POWS in terrible, cruel and painful circumstances.

According to a post–World War II protocol, American prisoners of war were never to break the chain of command, even in captivity. They were also never to provide to the enemy any information that might be harmful to their comrades. They were all in it together and, as the most senior, the 42-year-old Stockdale took command in the prison and turned the American soldiers and their captivity into a Stoic laboratory.

Everyone in the group was tortured—'endlessly'—and underwent lengthy and spirit-sapping periods of isolation. Stockdale was interrogated daily.

The first thing Stockdale did was use the control test to work out what he could or could not control in captivity. Within his power were 'opinions, my aims, my aversions, my own grief, my own joy, my judgements, my attitude about what is going on, my own good and my own evil'.

He then utilised the Stoic teachings of the preferred indifferents. Stockdale's station in life had been abruptly reduced from high to low (to 'an object of contempt') in that 30 seconds it took him to fall to earth. 'So make sure in your heart of hearts, in your inner self, that you treat your station in life with indifference, not with contempt, only with indifference,' he said.

The next Stoic challenge for Stockdale was around emotions. He recognised that his ordeal and the torture might never end, and that he needed to accept that it was happening. The people who were most broken (and this was also the case in concentration camps, according to an account by Primo Levi) were those who thought they would be rescued. Using negative visualisation, you needed to imagine that you wouldn't be. You also needed to confront the reality of your situation, without relying too much on hope. This is the attitude that Stockdale said was within his control. He later said in an interview with the writer Jim Collins, 'The optimists—oh, they were the ones who said, "We're going to be out by Christmas." And Christmas would come, and Christmas would go. Then they'd say, "We're going to be out by Easter." And Easter would come, and Easter would go. And then Thanksgiving, and then it would be Christmas again. And they died of a broken heart . . . This is a very important lesson. You must never confuse faith that you will prevail in the end—which you can never afford to lose—with the discipline to confront the most brutal facts of your current reality, whatever they might be.'

Stockdale endured the relentless harsh conditions in the prison by not looking too far into the future. 'I lived on a day-to-day basis,' wrote Stockdale in *Courage Under Fire*, in an echo of Epictetus, who said, 'Caretake this moment. Immerse yourself in its particulars. Respond to this person or that person, this challenge, this deed.'

The main aim for Stockdale was keeping self-respect even when the worst-case scenario was unfolding. Self-respect was within Stockdale's control. In order to keep self-respect in the camp, he had to not betray his country or his fellow soldiers; he had to have a good character.

After many years of torture and solitary confinement, as well as some of his men dying due to torture going too far, Stockdale was scheduled for another round of torture. He knew at that point that the pain would be of such intensity that he would not be able to contain the things that he should keep from the Vietcong. His character would then suffer as a result of the betrayals he made under torture. So in his cell, he smashed some glass and cut his wrists, intending to die rather than betray his character (in an echo of Cato). He was found by his captors and bandaged up. He was later rescued and enjoyed a distinguished career, dying at the age of 81 in 2005. Stockdale credits his survival in the camp—survival not just in body but also in terms of his self-respect, dignity and spirit—to Epictetus's teachings.

Cease to hope and you'll cease to fear

The bright, sunny flipside of anxiety is hope: projecting onto the future not a dark vision, but a hopeful one. Stockdale did not spend time in captivity living in hope that he would be freed; he just tried to live with dignity and respect in the small area that he could control. Likewise Primo Levi in Auschwitz kept his focus on daily survival: just trying to stay alive each day. 'To harbour desires inside the Lager [camp] is a mental death-sentence, as no desire will realistically be fulfilled. Therefore, to dwell on hunger and to hope for food is to subject oneself to mental torture as sufficient food will never be offered.'

The Stoics weren't fans of hope, seeing it as a form of wishful thinking—and a denying of reality and true clarity.

Seneca's friend Lucilius, to whom the *Moral Letters* was addressed, was a civil servant working in Sicily. One day Lucilius learned of a serious lawsuit against him that threatened to end his career and ruin his reputation. Distressed, he wrote to Seneca, who replied, 'You may expect that I will advise you to picture a happy outcome, and to rest in the allurements of hope' but 'I am going to conduct you to peace of mind through another route'. This culminated in the advice: 'If you wish to put off all worry, assume that what you fear may happen is certainly going to happen.'

In *Moral Letters to Lucilius*, Seneca famously wrote: 'Cease to hope and you will cease to fear.'

Hope and fear are two sides of the same coin. If you have a hope then you also have a fear that the hope will not be realised.

The price of peace of mind is the relinquishment of hope. And for Stoics, who prized tranquillity highly, it was a price they were more than willing to pay.

Say you hope not to get lung cancer despite being addicted to cigarettes (which you *shouldn't* be as a Stoic, because addiction messes with your rational mind, and the virtue of moderation—but bear with me). Every time you smoke, you hope you will be one of the lucky ones. But fear comes with this hope. If you hope for something not to happen then it stands to reason that you'll dread it happening. Who wants to live in dread? Better to live in reality.

A Stoic *would expect* to get sick one day if there was a strong link between cancer and smoking two packs of cigarettes a day. Her reason would tell her that is the case. She would light up not hoping to evade the statistics but looking reality in the face and expecting *not* to be one of the lucky ones. She would make a decision based on reality—and that reality might be—'I like smoking more than I value my long-term health.'

This Stoic can then say, 'I may have made a terrible decision but at least I wasn't fooling myself that I would be the exception who is spared serious illness.'

Recently I gave similar advice to a friend who was involved in complex commercial litigation that has lasted for many years. If he lost he would owe millions of dollars, his business would be shut down and he might face gaol time. 'Prepare for the worst,' I told him, echoing Seneca's advice to Lucilius.

'And hope for the best?' he said.

'No—just assume you will lose,' I replied. By assuming he will lose the case, he is then able to prepare himself should the worst happen. He'll be unafraid—or less afraid—of losing as he has adjusted his reality away from hope and towards the likelihood of a loss. He would then be more prepared mentally to start from scratch with no money, a trashed reputation or having done time in prison. All these things are undesirable—but being shocked and unprepared for them makes his situation even worse.

Part of giving up hope is the joy of being able to live firmly in the present rather than constantly thinking, dreading and fantasising about what might occur in the future.

You can never feel completely at ease when you have hope. You are placing your happiness in something that is outside your control. You can be let down terribly.

'*Cease to hope and you will cease to fear.*' Peace takes the place of hope and fear.

There is another good reason to ditch hope. When you remove hope from your life, you also remove its opposite: hopelessness. This is truly one of the worst human emotions. Nothing is as abject. It's a sibling of despair and creates its own dark fantasy—that is, the fantasy that you cannot recover, nothing will ever go right again, you will never succeed, your situation will never change and you are doomed.

Part 3

CRUNCH TIME

'Begin at once to live, and count each separate day as a separate life.'

—Seneca

'Look back over the past, with its changing empires that rose and fell, and you can foresee the future too.'

—Marcus Aurelius

It hits you without warning—the middle ages. I'm in my forties—how did that happen? Suddenly and gradually, I suppose. But the question of how best to spend my days was becoming more pressing as the years went on. Time began to feel more finite. The question of waste started to haunt me.

There are the late night, early morning pangs of dreams unrealised and paths not taken, opportunities that may not come around again, lives not lived. I'll probably never relocate to Paris and work in a bookshop. My life at this point has taken a shape. Some things start to look fixed—for better or worse.

Then there is a deeper shadow of the more permanent losses still to come—the whole chain of it, acquaintances, mentors, parents, friends—gone, gone, gone . . . this chain leading ultimately to one's own death. And death, in our society that worships youth, is the thing we don't know how to talk about.

Amid the reckoning of personal losses, there are the bigger losses of systems.

These systems are ecological and social: they are the clean air in cities, and the bright colours of the Great Barrier Reef, they are healthy river networks and the brilliance of butterflies, they are beaches before they erode or get eaten by tides. My travels in recent years have slammed me into systems collapses—seen with my own eyes. There was snorkelling among the bleached tombstone shapes of dying coral reefs, and taking small sips of thin breath in Delhi—where the air quality was so bad it broke all previous measures and a rickshaw ride left me with eyes and throat streaming. There was trying but failing to walk on eroded beaches, or swim in water that had once been pristine but was now dirty and filled with rubbish.

To be fully, vibrantly alive is to also be in grief. And so that is where we shall go now.

How to . . .

Grieve

'What need is there to weep over parts of life? The whole of it calls for tears.'
—Seneca

'Receive without conceit, release without struggle.'
—Marcus Aurelius

S ince starting on this journey exploring ancient wisdom, the one thing I've been most asked about the most is the Stoic response to grief or loss of a loved one. People in grief feel marooned, without a map or guidance on the path through, and wonder if the works of the ancient Stoics offer any consolation.

Hmm . . . do they offer consolation? The answer is yes and no. The Stoics thought and wrote a lot about grief. But when asked, I'm hesitant to give a bereft person Stoic advice for grieving when they are in the middle of that distressing and disorienting process. It takes a lifetime of practice to grieve like a Stoic, and it's a process that is much misunderstood. For the uninitiated, the Stoic approach to grief can come across as being too harsh—brutal, even. But for those who have studied and practised Stoicism, the approach is consistent with the entire philosophy. It's empowering and wise.

So while I do recommend the Stoic approach to grief, ideally you would learn how to grieve like a Stoic before the people you love start to die.

Grieve your loved ones while they are alive

The first step of grieving your loved ones before they die is to visualise them dying, see the funeral and practise delivering a eulogy in your head. By practising the eulogy in your head, or even making some notes about it in your journal, you will recall all the great and positive traits about the person you are mourning. How exciting and wonderful then to meet with that person and they are still alive (for now). You will come away with a renewed sense of gratitude about that person's uniqueness and your relationship with them.

We covered negative visualisation in the chapter 'How to be Mortal'. Negative visualisation, practised fleetingly, will allow you to get used to the idea that people we love won't be around forever, and will allow you a mental rehearsal of what it would be like to get the news that they are dead or attend their funeral. These thoughts would strike most people as unpleasant, but since they are actually likely to happen in the future, then it is good to give yourself some sort of emotional vaccine by imagining them dead.

HAVE GRATITUDE

A by-product of mourning people while they are still alive is to appreciate them more now, while you can. Don't leave things unsaid; don't neglect a friendship or familial relationship; properly enjoy your time with people. Don't spend time with a friend or your kids only to be distracted by your phone.

Epictetus counselled that we can lose friends not only through death but through disputes or a change in circumstances. So we need to make the most of our friends while we have them around.

We should also be grateful for our own life. Just as our friends can suddenly die or die before they get to old age, so can we. Everything we enjoy, we should anticipate coming to an end. You don't want to wait until it's too late to enjoy the world and all it has to offer. It's like the final scene in *Don't Look Up*, when Leonardo DiCaprio's character, Randall, says to the table of his family and friends, 'We really did have everything, didn't we?' Just as he says it, a deadly comet hits and everything on earth is obliterated. Don't wait until the very last moment on earth before you realise that you 'really did have everything'.

We are less likely to squander time if we realise it is a finite resource.

How to grieve the Stoic way

On his exile to the island of Corsica, Seneca wrote a letter of condolence to his friend Marcia, who had been mourning the death of her young adult son Metilius for over three years. This letter shows Seneca as a therapist but also as a barrister, litigating a number of arguments as to why Marcia's grief must end. The letter is remarkable, and still feels fresh and useful today to anyone facing grief.

The first paragraphs lay out Marcia's issue and Seneca's reasoning for her emotions not being allowed to harden into something chronic and immoveable.

> Three whole years have now passed, and yet the first violence of your sorrow has in no way abated. Your grief is renewed and grows stronger every day—by lingering it has established its right to stay, and has now reached the point that it is ashamed to make an end; just as all vices become deep-rooted unless they are crushed when they spring up, so, too, such a state of sadness and wretchedness, with its self-afflicted torture, feeds at last upon its very bitterness, and the grief of an unhappy mind becomes a morbid pleasure. And so I should have liked to approach your cure in the first stages of your sorrow. While it was still young, a gentler remedy might have been used to check its violence; against inveterate evils the fight must be more vehement.
>
> This is likewise true of wounds—they are easy to heal while they are still fresh and bloody. When they have festered and turned into a wicked sore, then they must be cauterised and, opened up to the very bottom, must submit to probing fingers. As it is, I cannot possibly be a match for such hardened grief by being considerate and gentle; it must be crushed.

Seneca believed Marcia needed to draw a line under her sorrow. If she continued to grieve she would be removed 'from the number of the living'.

He warned her he would use a firm tone: 'Let others use soft measures and caresses; I have determined to do battle with your grief, and I will dry those weary and exhausted eyes, which already, to tell you the truth, are weeping more from habit than from sorrow.'

He counselled Marcia to practise self-restraint in grief so that she would not suffer twice. The first suffering was the actual death of her son and the second was the prolonged period of grieving.

Wrote Seneca, 'For what madness it is—how monstrous!—to punish one's self for misfortune and add new ill to present ills!'

This way of thinking about suffering should be familiar to us now. The Stoics—far from being anti-joy—were actually anti–needless suffering. They tried to *avoid suffering* in situations where it was avoidable.

Other sons died, so yours can too

Seneca, in his letter, attempted to convince Marcia that the death of her son, while tragic, should not have been a surprise. After all, she knew of other young men who had died, so why should her own son not die?

It is a maxim that echoes Epictetus who said: 'When somebody's wife or child dies, to a man we say, "Well, that's part of life." But if one of our own family is involved, then right away it's "Poor, poor me!" We would do better to remember how we react when a similar loss afflicts others.'

This is true today as it was 2000 years ago. We see bad things happening all around us—people getting sick and dying all the time, yet we are shocked when it happens to us or people we are close to. It's as if we believe we are immune from death. (*I wish we could have our old life back. We had the greatest economy that we've ever had, and we didn't have death.*') We also have a similar disconnect when it comes to the climate crisis. We theoretically know that we are headed in a bad direction, but extinction or climate collapse doesn't seem quite real to us.

But as we learned in earlier chapters, part of taking action in this world, and mitigating suffering for yourself and others, is to actually *be in reality.*

Seneca tried to take us there. He asked, in a similar vein to Epictetus:

> How many funerals pass our houses? Yet we do not think of death. How many untimely deaths? We think only of our son's coming of age, of his service in the army, or of his succession to his father's estate. How many rich men suddenly sink into poverty before our very eyes, without it ever occurring to our minds that our own wealth is exposed to exactly the same risks? When, therefore, misfortune befalls us, we cannot help collapsing all the more completely, because we are struck.

The control test and grief

Seneca counselled Marcia, 'one should not be upset by uncontrollable events'. If you think back to the control test, you cannot control when someone, including yourself (unless by their own hand), dies. As a result, you should not grieve excessively because you do not want to be injured twice by mourning something that is out of your control to fix.

Using reason when grieving

The Stoics were not against grieving; they wanted to avoid *excessive* grieving. When a natural time for grieving has come to a close, we can use judgements and reason to assess that the time is right to move on, and then act accordingly. This is to protect our own wellbeing and mental health. Seneca believed that Marcia had let her grief go on too long, beyond what was a reasonable time to grieve. He told Marcia that even her friends were awkward and didn't know how to handle her prolonged grief or what to say to her anymore.

'I pray and beseech you not to be self-willed and beyond the management of your friends. You must be aware that none of them know how to behave . . .'

He gave the example of two other mothers who were grieving. Octavia never ceased being in grief—and neglected her surviving family and other duties.

But the other mother, Livia, 'she at last laid [her son Drusus] in the tomb, she left her sorrow there with him, and grieved no more than was becoming to a Caesar or due to a son'.

Seneca told Marcia that she had two alternatives:

Choose, therefore, which of these two examples you think the more commendable: if you prefer to follow the former, you will remove yourself from the number of the living . . . If, on the other hand, showing a milder and better regulated spirit, you try to follow the example of the latter most exalted lady, you will not be in misery, nor will you wear your life out with suffering.

Using the virtues to get you through turmoil

A well-practised Stoic (as you are now) will be aware of the four virtues and will have spent time honing them. These virtues are like superpowers that can assist you as you meet various challenges in life—including grief. With wisdom and courage, you can find the strength to overcome the loss, while also being able to place your loss in the context of life, where everything is mortal, and subject to the cycle of birth and death. The virtue of temperance or moderation will also allow you to act with awareness of when your grief is too heightened or the opposite happens and you become too numbed out. Just as Aristotle's golden mean applies to a variety of emotions and events in life, it also applies to grief, 'for there is such a thing as moderation even in grieving,' wrote Seneca.

Using judgement when it comes to grief

In Part 1, in the chapter 'How to be Untroubled', we learned the Stoic response to passions. The Stoics said that, essentially, we have control over our emotions except for initial impressions (such as jumping when being startled, blushing when embarrassed), and so, grief, after the initial shock of the death, is within our control to manage.

When he talked about managing grief, Seneca was not recommending that all emotions be suppressed and there be no crying. The Stoics thought it normal and natural to cry when someone had died—with the tears arising from shock, sorrow, loss and also joy at happy memories. What they cautioned against was grief that was performative and over the top, grief that went on too long, or disbelief that someone had died.

In his *Letter to Marcia*, Seneca said that it is natural to grieve, and also natural to feel shock when someone dies. In his own life he was shocked when his young friend Annaeus Serenus died. Seneca said, 'I am writing these things to you—I, who wept for my beloved Annaeus Serenus so unrestrainedly I understand, now, that the main reason I felt such grief was that I had never thought it possible that his death should precede my own. I kept in mind only that he was younger than I, much younger. As if birth order determined our fate!' But he concluded, 'Whatever can happen at any time, can happen today.' And it can happen to anyone, of any age, even people younger than you. *As if birth order determined our fate!*

As the Stoics practised their whole lives for the eventuality of people they loved dying, they expected not to be shocked by the deaths of their friends and family, and not to suffer twice by undergoing a prolonged and painful period of mourning.

Everything is on loan

Seneca reminded Marcia that all we have is 'on loan' from fortune who can reclaim it whenever she wants—without advance notice. 'We should love all of our dear ones but always with the thought that we have no promise that we may keep them forever—nay, no promise even that we may keep them for long.'

Seneca also reminded Marcia of the unspoken pact or price for our life here on earth: 'It is our duty always to be able to lay our hands upon what has been lent us with no fixed date for its return, and to restore it when called upon without a murmur: the most detestable kind of debtor is he who rails at his creditor.'

Better to have loved and have lost . . .

Another of Seneca's key messages to Marcia was that it was better to be thankful for what she had, rather than resentful for what she had lost. '"But," say you, "it might have lasted longer." True, but you have been better dealt with than if you had never had a son, for, supposing you were given your choice, which is the better lot, to be happy for a short time or not at all?'

This is a version of 'it's better to have loved and lost than not loved at all'.

Seneca himself had a son who died when he was a baby, twenty days before Seneca's exile to Corsica. The child died in the arms of his grandmother, Helvia—Seneca's mother—'as she showered the baby with kisses'. Marcus Aurelius and his wife Faustina had at least fourteen children but only four girls and one boy outlived Aurelius, which meant he had to cope with the loss of nine of his children. The child mortality rate in ancient times was shocking, and may account for some of their need to fortify themselves around the death of children—but many of these lessons are still applicable today (and will be applicable as long as humans are mortal).

No such thing as dying too soon

We are fond of saying almost unthinkingly that someone who died young 'died too soon'. But the Stoics challenged this notion. They did not believe in 'too soon' (partly because of their beliefs around fate).

Both Seneca and Marcus Aurelius wrote about the waste of those who lived but were not alive in the proper sense of the word. They worked too much, chased money or fame, or acted as if they had many lives to live so they did not get started on the one they were living now. These people may have lived until they were 90, but the Stoics believed it was better to live until you were 25 and have a life filled with meaning and virtue than a stale, long life. 'Life, it is thanks to Death that I hold thee so dear. Think how great a blessing is a timely death, how many have been injured by living longer than they ought,' wrote Seneca.

Seneca gave the examples of statesmen—like Gnaeus Pompeius—who lived past their peak and ended their life in disgrace or by betrayal. We always assume that when life has been cut short it is a tragedy and has deprived us of a number of good things, but this is by no means assured. Sometimes death is actually a blessing.

'To each man a varying length of days has been assigned: no one dies before his time, because he was not destined to live any longer than he did . . . We all fall into this mistake of supposing that it is only old men, already in the decline of life, who are drawing near to death, whereas our first infancy, our youth, indeed every time of life leads thither,' wrote Seneca.

Being dead is just the same as before we were born

The Stoics didn't believe in hell, so being dead wasn't a bad thing; it was neutral. They compared it to not being born. You can't remember what life was like before you arrived on the scene, and it will be the same when you die. There is no emotion attached to not being here on earth, because you are not around to feel anything. 'Death is neither a good nor a bad thing, for that alone which is something can be a good or a bad thing: but that which is nothing, and reduces all things to nothing, does not hand us over to either fortune, because good and bad require some material to work upon,' wrote Seneca.

There is an echo of this in the teachings of Epicurus: 'Death does not concern us, because as long as we exist, death is not here. And when it does come, we no longer exist.'

Nothing in life comes with a guarantee

Unlike a product that we can hand back if it's faulty—or the replaceable nature of so many of our consumer goods—life is the one thing we cannot replace, and the Stoics said we should be aware of this. In particular they say that when we have children we are making a bargain with nature that the child can be returned (die) at any time, not of our choosing but of the choosing of nature. And how that child may turn out is not guaranteed either.

Seneca said:

> To everyone Nature says: 'I do not deceive any person. If you choose to have children . . . one of them may perhaps prove the saviour of his country, or perhaps its betrayer . . . If you still choose to rear children, after I have explained these conditions to you, you render yourself incapable of blaming the gods, for they never guaranteed anything to you.'

In fact the only guarantee is that 'we are born into a world of things which are all destined to die,' wrote Seneca. 'We have entered the kingdom of Fortune, whose rule is harsh and unconquerable, and at her whim we will endure suffering, deserved and undeserved.'

To die is to know life's final big mystery

None of us know what happens when we die, except those who are dead (ignoring the lack of consciousness that actually being dead entails— so there is no 'I' to know the mysteries . . . but let's go with it for now).

Seneca, in trying to convince Marcia to stop her excessive grieving, wrote:

> the inhabited world . . . in huge conflagration it will burn and scorch and burn all mortal things . . . stars will clash with stars and all the fiery matter of the world . . . will blaze up in a common conflagration. Then the souls of the Blessed, who have partaken of immortality, when it will seem best for god to create the universe anew . . . will be changed again into our former elements. Happy, Marcia, is your son who knows these mysteries!

Marcus Aurelius and Seneca both wrote about being returned to the elements when they die, and the cyclical nature of life and death.

History does not tell us whether Marcia was actually consoled by Seneca's letter and was able to put his arguments into action. But his remarkable letter survives, and those of us who are lucky enough not to be grieving right now can consult its timeless wisdom as a 'how to' guide for when the season for grieving comes.

The Stoic approach to grief is a vibe

I explained the Stoic approach to death while walking over the dunes towards the beach to a friend whose mother had died six months before. And I explained it over a drink to another friend whose mother had died twelve months before. Both times I was met with a bewildered silence. This did not jibe with their lived experiences of grief, which they both described as not being amenable to reason or even linear time. They talked about grief arriving in waves of emotion (emotion that was very hard to control before it came on, like trying to hold back a wave in the ocean) and taking its own time hitting and receding, hitting and receding. They spoke of strange dreams, and the anguish on waking to discover their beloved was still dead. They spoke of feeling, you know, fine, it was all fine— before they'd remember their mother was dead, and they'd fall apart. The notion that rationality could be used to temper grief seemed strange to them.

American poet Edna St Vincent Millay wrote a short poem about prolonged grief:

Time does not bring relief; you all have lied
Who told me time would ease me of my pain!
I miss him in the weeping of the rain;
I want him at the shrinking of the tide . . .

Would the Stoic technique of grieving while the loved one was still alive 'ease me of my pain'? Seneca's advice seemed like a psychological trick—a device designed to deceive the sore and tender heart with a clever head.

Seneca's approach to grief has fallen out of favour since the time of the Roman Stoics. It is now seen as highly insensitive and very wrong to hurry people along in their grief. Discussing Stoicism with newly bereaved friends, I felt a weird sort of awkwardness, even embarrassment just describing the Stoic approach to grief.

In the course of writing this book, I've been lucky enough not to go through the grieving process, so I cannot bring my personal experience to bear on this important aspect of Stoicism. I have been doing a lot of negative visualisation though, and hope that, when the time comes (as it will, over and over and over again—unless I die first), I can grieve like a Stoic.

Resilience and grief

Modern Stoic William Irvine wrote that there was a shift in bereavement practices around 1969 with the publication of *On Death and Dying*, by Elisabeth Kübler-Ross, outlining the five stages of grief. This influential work said that we move through defined stages when we have a loss: denial, anger, bargaining, depression and, finally, acceptance.

The Stoics—including Irvine—would advise that you skip the early stages and go straight to acceptance, as, once someone has died, you can't do anything about it, so you may as well accept it so as not to cause further disturbance to yourself.

Irvine wrote about how you should avoid making yourself a victim, even if you are the subject of an injustice. Your reaction to situations, including grief, is within the field of your control. 'Being a victim, after all, relieves you of responsibility for many aspects of your life that have gone wrong. It also entitles you to special treatment: victims need time and space in which to recover . . . At the same time, playing the role of victim is likely to increase the anguish you experience as a result of the wrongs that are done to you,' he wrote.

Resilience, and the Stoic virtue of courage, can help you overcome setbacks, including the death of people you love, and make the most of the good things in your life.

When it comes to grief, the Stoics didn't say that we shouldn't feel sad when someone we love dies. After all, that is a natural feeling. Seneca said, 'Nature requires from us some sorrow.' But we should not prolong the grief more than is natural. The Stoics saw ulterior motives in grief, including guilt for not spending more time with the dead person while they were still alive. Or they saw excessive grief as virtue signalling or a show of how sensitive and tender-hearted the mourner was. Or they saw it as a way of attracting the attention and care of others. This is a bit cynical but there is also a small measure of truth in it. When we grieve, others are kinder to us, and show us more care, affection, understanding, lenience and tenderness. It feels good to be loved in this way, and treated carefully. But maybe it's a sign that we should treat each other lovingly all the time.

Die

'The final hour when we cease to exist does not itself bring death; it merely of itself completes the death-process. We reach death at that moment, but we have been a long time on the way.'

—Seneca

'What is death? A scary mask. Take it off—see, it doesn't bite. Eventually, body and soul will have to separate, just as they existed separately before we were born. So why be upset if it happens now? If it isn't now, it's later.'

—Epictetus

'What we do now echoes in eternity.'

—Marcus Aurelius

I know it's just a philosophy (one of many)—and it's based on reason not faith, and there are no gods in this realm, and no saints. There are no rituals and there are no sacraments. There's no church or temple or shala or mosque or cathedral or altar or holy house or tabernacle. There are no real earthly emissaries: no priests, cardinals, bishops, imams, rabbis, nuns, preachers or clergy of any kind.

There is also no real holy book—just a diary one man wrote for himself centuries ago (shelved like any ordinary book in the Penguin classics), a few earlier fragments in ancient Greek, some speeches, plays and lectures recorded by hand and passed down and down and down (730,000 days and nights) . . .

For me, what began as a purely intellectual journey in 2018 alchemised into something that felt more spiritual. Throughout the uncertainty and pain and wonder of the last four years, Stoicism was sometimes a comforting companion, sometimes a tough, almost harsh teacher. But I did not once doubt the truth of it, the comfort of its consolations, the hard unyielding wisdom contained in ancient sentences that read like poetry and were powerful and true enough to break my heart.

Purists will wince, but how can I explain that over time Stoicism changed everything from my view of nature both human and the cosmos, to my understanding of reality, my place in the world, my relationship and duty to others, and how I approached death and mortality?

Stoicism, for me, bridged the realms of the intellectual, the emotions and the spirit. It integrated all of them. The philosophy was teaching me how to live, and part of that was also to teach me how to die.

'You are a little soul carrying around a corpse,' said Epictetus: once again not mincing his words; once again, calling it.

We have already discussed many of the Stoic teachings on death and mortality, but it is worth returning to the key messages.

Everything—even our own life—is on loan and must be returned

It was September 2019 in western Mongolia and our group was spending two weeks travelling and meeting with various nomadic tribes. One afternoon we met an elderly nomad on the side of a hill. Tio had a face like Samuel Beckett and eyes the colour of amber. Moving lightly up a rockface, he showed us some ancient petroglyphs of alpine ibexes in the nearby caves and told us his life story. As he was talking about the cycles of his life, which closely followed that of the seasons and the animals, I wondered about some of the practicalities of being a nomad. Where—for example—do they bury their dead? If you are constantly moving, if you don't belong to a place, where are the cemeteries?

Tio put his hand on his heart. We bury our dead here, he told me, thumping his chest. You never really die if you live on in someone's memory. Your community, your friends, your family—they are a living memorial to you. It's that spirit living on in others that is your legacy, your animating force. Your body is irrelevant once you die. And so, the nomads leave the corpses of their kin behind when they set off again, down the mountain when the cold sets in, or up above when the snows have melted.

The bodies are left to be feasted on by animals and birds of prey. Tio seemed pleased with this situation; after all, the nomads had been hunting animals their whole lives, and so to replenish the system that had nourished them seemed fitting.

This way of life reminded me of the ancient Stoics. The Mongolian nomads believed that death is natural, and when you die, you are returned to nature. In some of the Stoic literature they didn't call it 'death'; they called it 'being returned'.

Part of the acceptance of death occurring—squaring up to our mortality and the mortality of others—is the idea that our time here on earth is brief. Embedded in Stoic philosophy is the notion that we don't own things or people; they are on loan from the universe.

In his journal, Marcus Aurelius wrote: 'All that is harmony for you, my Universe, is in harmony with me as well. Nothing that comes at the right time for you is too early or too late for me. Everything is fruit to me that your seasons bring, Nature. All things come from you, have their being in you, and return to you.'

Don't make a scene when it comes to dying

Seneca wrote about how he overcomes fear of death in a letter to Lucilius. It's to do with rehearsing thoughts of one's death. He said:

> Rehearse this thought every day, that you may be able to depart from life contentedly; for many men clutch and cling to life, even as those who are carried down a rushing stream clutch and cling to briars and sharp rocks. Most men ebb and flow in wretchedness between the fear of death and the hardships of life; they are unwilling to live, and yet they do not know how to die. For this reason, make life as a whole agreeable to yourself by banishing all worry about it.

What Seneca was essentially saying was that you are going to die anyway but you do have a choice about whether you are content when you leave (like having enjoyed a great holiday and checking out of

283

your nice hotel with a smile on your face) or in absolute agony and denial (refusing to leave your hotel room when the holiday ends and being violently ejected by security).

Death—when it arrives and the manner in which it does so—is out of our control. But our fear of death and our reaction to it is very much in our control.

If we realise we are going to die and then stop worrying about it, not only will we have a more relaxed life, but we will also have a more relaxed death. Interestingly, while the manner of Seneca's death was far from relaxed, he himself seemed almost leisurely as he attempted to die.

After Nero's henchmen came knocking at his door to order Seneca to kill himself, the old philosopher accepted his fate. First, in an echo of Socrates's death he drank hemlock, and when that didn't work he cut a vein, then cut his knees and legs. And when that didn't work—due to his age and frugal diet perhaps—he got his servants to draw him a bath so he could asphyxiate himself on the steam. All the while, he was surrounded by his wife and friends, whom he comforted (he also talked his wife out of killing herself) and told them to accept his death, as he had accepted it. Seneca had spent his whole adult life preparing for the moments of his death—and this training had made him calm and unafraid.

What happens when we die?

In life—and in this book—once again we come full circle from the beginning. Just as we started as nothing, so when we die, we are returned to nature, our bodies becoming matter or material to be reabsorbed into the earth (ashes to ashes/dust to dust).

Epictetus wrote of death, 'Every part of me then will be reduced by change into some part of the universe, and that again will change into another part of the universe, and so on forever.'

Marcus Aurelius, who wrote a lot about death, said, 'Accept death in a cheerful spirit, as nothing but the dissolution of the elements from which each living thing is composed. If it doesn't hurt the individual elements to change continually into one another, why are people afraid of all of them changing and separating? It's a natural thing. And nothing natural is evil.'

Death is a central organising principle in Stoicism. The Stoics always kept it in mind because knowing there would be no second shot at life allowed them to live it fully. After all, we die every day— and all the days we have lived up to now are 'already in the hands of death'.

The process takes a lifetime but the destination is never in doubt. We'll leave the last words to Marcus Aurelius:

Just that you do the right thing. The rest doesn't matter. Cold or warm. Tired or well-rested. Despised or honoured. Dying . . . or busy with other assignments. Because dying, too, is one of our assignments in life. There as well: 'To do what needs doing.' Look inward. Don't let the true nature of anything elude you. Before long, all existing things will be transformed, to rise like smoke (assuming all things become one), or be dispersed in fragments . . . to move from one unselfish act to another with God in mind. Only there, delight and stillness . . . when jarred, unavoidably, by circumstances, revert at once to yourself, and don't lose the rhythm more than you can help. You'll have a better grasp of the harmony if you keep going back to it.

Epilogue

ood news! It was April 2022, and my friend Jo had finished her cancer treatments and received the all clear from her doctors. I asked her if she'd got anything out of the bite-sized Stoicism lessons.

She had!

'Even apart from the content, having the voice notes from a friend when you're isolated in a hospital was so fortifying, and broke up the terrible loneliness of the situation,' she told me. 'But the message also resonated. So much of the advice and counsel you get when you get cancer is well intentioned but falls into the category of toxic positivity. "You've got this", "Kick cancer's arse", "Stay positive", etc. This is so useless, and makes you feel bad for feeling bad. It assigns you a level of control you simply don't have. The flipside of this is the real despair you can feel when confronted with pain, and fear, and the sense of impending loss. I liked the Stoicism because it trod a middle path—acknowledging that suffering exists, that it's part of life, and that it can be endured.'

As for me, I'm still using Stoicism every day.

Firstly, I use Stoicism and its techniques simply to get through the day and cope with negative feelings and situations that would otherwise depress or overwhelm me.

Second, I use Stoicism to regulate my behaviour towards others. This includes becoming less reactive, less angry, less judgemental, less bitter and less aggrieved. In short, it chills me out. In 2019, when I got properly stuck into Stoicism, I began to let go of a lot of stuff that would have otherwise pissed me off or agitated me—and that process is ongoing.

Third, Stoicism helps me refine my emotional goals. Instead of striving to be happy, I was introduced to the subtler and potentially more achievable goal of being tranquil.

Happiness—at least in my case—is often a fleeting emotion that seemingly comes and goes on a whim (and leaves me chasing its tail, begging for just one more hour in the warm pool of its sun). By contrast, tranquillity, although a less exciting state, is more constant, acting like a slow-release drug that keeps me stable and content throughout the day. Tranquillity promises ongoing freedom from distress and worry. Don't we all want that?

Fourth, I use Stoicism to draw a boundary between the things I should worry about (or concern myself with) and those that I should leave alone. Once the distinction has been made, I do not ruminate over things I can't control. (Or at least I try not to. This is not a way of thinking that comes automatically.) This boundary really is a life-saver and embodies the radical promise of Stoicism.

Fifth, I use Stoicism as a guide to what constitutes being a Good Person, living a Good Life. And although I only sometimes live up to the ideals, I now have a really clear sense of the parameters of what a decent person is and the component parts of a good life. (Spoiler: a Good Life as envisioned by the Stoics is not the sort of Good Life we are sold under late capitalism in the 21st century.)

Sixth, I continue to re-evaluate my relationship with time and also with death, and realise the two are strongly linked. It's impossible to make a committed study of Stoicism without fully squaring with your mortality. And not just your own mortality, but the appalling, deep, unavoidable truth that all the people you love will die. When you fully square with the fact that you and your loved ones are going to die, then you begin to view time differently. It suddenly becomes apparent what a precious and finite resource it is. You won't want to waste a minute.

Seventh, I am re-evaluating and recalibrating my relationships with externals such as money, a healthy body, reputation, fame and possessions. I use the Stoic concept of 'preferred indifferents' to reframe these as things to view with nonchalance.

And finally, I use aspects of Stoicism's teachings on nature and the cosmos to frame my sense of wonder at the natural world without resorting to a theist position that all this beauty must have been the work of the hand of God.

These realisations have been a number of years in the making. Once you have them, the hard work is just beginning. The Stoic practice is daily. Stoicism—like religion, like the Catholicism of my youth—requires a dedicated practice to keep the muscle strong. If months went past and I didn't read a Stoic text or schedule a Stoic walk with Andrew, I would find my practice of the philosophy slipping and I would fall back into old habits and patterns. I would fret about things that were not in my control, I would forget about tranquillity and set about chasing old highs, ignoring the fact that they always swung back into the old low lows. I would be enticed by externals—possessions and fame and reputation and appearance. Anxiety would creep back. Time would be wasted.

I'd forget all that I'd learned—and then, just before despair clicked in, I would remember that I had all the tools I needed in the bag at my feet. Like a penitent back at the doors of the church or a lapsed exerciser returning chastened with their soft muscles to the gym, I found that Stoicism was something I could recommit to (in fact, must recommit to) over and over and over and over again.

When I found myself in tough places over the last few years, I kept returning to the Stoics. 'Though you break your heart, men will go on as before,' wrote Marcus Aurelius, his voice intimate and close—like you were reading his private diary.

So you keep going. Just keep going.

Acknowledgements

Thanks to all the friends who acted as Stoicism guinea pigs over the past few years, graciously accepting advice that began with 'Well, the Stoics would say . . .'

To my pals who encouraged me to keep going with this project when it had its difficult moments—thank you.

My gratitude to friends who read various versions of this book and provided excellent advice: Michael Safi, Matthew Goldberg, Lee Glendinning, Denis Mooney, Stu Spiers and Hal Crawford.

To Bridie Jabour for her suggestions on structure, Adam Wesselinoff for our conversations interrogating Stoicism, Jo Tovey for our Stoicism WhatsApp chats—and for sharing some of her story here. To my parents for their enthusiasm for this project—in particular, my mother, Mary Delaney, for sharing with me her knowledge on early Christianity.

To my publisher, Kelly Fagan, who saw many years ago that Stoicism would be needed in modern times; my agent Pippa Masson for being a great sounding board for all the iterations of this book; and AC, fellow Stoic traveller.

Further reading

David Fideler, *Breakfast with Seneca: A Stoic guide to the art of living*, W.W. Norton & Co., 2021

Ryan Holiday and Stephen Hanselman, *Lives of the Stoics*, Profile Books, 2020

William B. Irvine, *A Guide to the Good Life: The ancient art of Stoic joy*, Oxford University Press, 2008

William B. Irvine, *The Stoic Challenge: A philosopher's guide to becoming tougher, calmer, and more resilient*, W.W. Norton & Co., 2019

Martha Nussbaum, *The Therapy of Desire: Theory and practice in Hellenistic ethics*, Princeton University Press, 2018

Massimo Pigliucci, *How to Be a Stoic: Ancient wisdom for modern living*, Penguin Random House, 2017

Donald Robertson, *Stoicism and the Art of Happiness*, Hodder Education, 2013

James Romm, *Dying Every Day: Seneca at the court of Nero*, Random House, 2014

John Sellars, *Lessons in Stoicism: What ancient philosophers teach us about how to live*, Allen Lane, 2019

John Sellars, *Stoicism*, Routledge, 2014

James Stockdale, *Courage Under Fire: Testing Epictetus's doctrines in a laboratory of human behavior*, Hoover Institution Press, 1993

Emily Wilson, *Seneca: A life*, Penguin, 2016

Donna Zuckerberg, *Not All Dead White Men: Classics and misogyny in the digital age*, Harvard University Press, 2018

About the Author

BRIGID DELANEY is a political speechwriter for Australia's minister for finance and minister for women. For many years she wrote the popular weekly column Brigid Delaney's Diary for the *Guardian*. She cocreated the Netflix series *Wellmania*, based on her last book, and cofounded the anti–death penalty movement Mercy Campaign. She lives in Australia.